W9-ADX-918

mustsees
Montreal &
Quebec City

St. Lawrence River and Biosphère Canada on St. Helen's Island, Montreal
© Philippe Renault/hemis.fr

mustsees **Montreal & Quebec City**

Editorial Manager	Jonathan P. Gilbert
Contributing Writer	Gregory B. Gallagher
Production Manager	Natasha G. George
Cartography	Peter Wrenn
Photo Editor	Yoshimi Kanazawa
Photo Researcher	Nicole D. Jordan
Proofreaders	Jane Donovan
Layout	Alison Rayner, Natasha G. George
Interior Design	Chris Bell, cbdesign
Cover Design	Chris Bell, cbdesign, Natasha G. George

Contact Us

Michelin Travel and Lifestyle
One Parkway South
Greenville, SC 29615
USA
www.michelintravel.com
michelin.guides@us.michelin.com

Michelin TravelPartner
Hannay House
39 Clarendon Road
Watford, Herts WD17 1JA
UK
(01923) 205 240
www.ViaMichelin.com
travelpubsales@uk.michelin.com

Special Sales

For information regarding bulk sales, customized
editions and premium sales, please contact
our Customer Service Departments:

USA	1-800-432-6277
UK	(01923) 205 240
Canada	1-800-361-8236

Michelin Apa Publications Ltd

A joint venture between Michelin and Langenscheidt

58 Borough High Street, London SE1 1XF, United Kingdom

No part of this publication may be reproduced in any form
without the prior permission of the publisher.

© 2011 Michelin Apa Publications Ltd
ISBN 978-1-907099-37-3
Printed: August 2011
Printed and bound: Himmer, Germany

Note to the reader:

Welcome to Montreal & Quebec City

Rue Saint-Louis, Upper Town, Quebec City

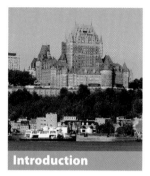

Introduction

p29

p112

p87

TABLE OF CONTENTS

★★★ ATTRACTIONS

Unmissable historic, cultural, and natural sights

Old Montreal p 37
©Richard Nowitz/Apa Publications

Montreal Botanical Garden p 70
©Montreal Botanical Garden_Michel Tremblay

Mount Royal Park p 71
©Juliane Martini/Michelin

Montreal Botanical Garden p 70

Quebec City, Lower Town p 80
©Mary Lane/Bigstockphoto.com

Biosphère Canada, Montreal   p 62

©Juliane Martini/Michelin

Quebec City   p 76

© Tibor Bognár/Age Fotostock

Notre-Dame Basilica, Montreal   p 44

©A. Korzekwa/iStockphoto.com

★★★ ATTRACTIONS

Unmissable historic, cultural, and natural sights

For more than 75 years, travelers have used the Michelin stars to take the guesswork out of planning a trip. Our star-rating system helps you make the best decision on where to go, what to do, and what to see. A three-star rating means it's one of the "absolutelys," two stars indicates it's one of the "should sees," and one star says it's one of the "sees"—a must if you have the time.

★★★	Absolutely Must See
★★	Really Must See
★	Must See
No Star	See

MUST KNOW

ACTIVITIES

Unmissable activities, entertainment, restaurants, and hotels

French Canadians are famous for their passionate recipe of mixing family, outdoor, and culinary activities. Enjoying life is the widespread ambiance here in La Belle Province. *Look-out for the Michelin Man throughout the guide for the top activities.*

Outings

Festivals

Hotels

Nightlife

Relax

Restaurants

Shopping

Sports

Fun

STAR ATTRACTIONS

CALENDAR OF EVENTS

Listed below is a selection of Montreal's most popular annual events. Note that dates may vary from year to year. For more detailed information, contact Tourisme Québec *(514-873-2015 or 877-266-5687; www.bonjourquebec.com) or Tourisme Montréal (www.tourisme-montreal.org).*

January

Fête des Neiges
Parc Jean-Drapeau, Île Ste-Hélène *(www.fetedesneiges.com)* The definitive Montreal winter festival for the whole family attracts legions of visitors for a wide range of outdoor activity fun on the site of Expo-67 World's Fair.

IglooFest (mid-Jan for 14 days)
(www.igloofest.ca) This frenzied outdoor winter rave attracts an international gathering of electronic live music DJs and musicians, plus an original igloo village architectural concept.

February

Festival Montréal en Lumière (Montreal High Lights Festival)
Various locations *(www.montrealhighlights.com)* Combines a unique indoor/outdoor program of culinary tastings, gourmet workshops, local eatery deals, world-class entertainment, and nightly fireworks to warm.

Rendez-Vous du Cinéma Québécois (Festival of Quebec Films)
Various locations *(www.rvcq.com)* Since 1982 this film festival presents the cultural, educational, and professional inside look at Quebec films.

March

International Film Festivals
Various locations Three major film festivals in Montreal during March celebrate art, children, and AmerAsia themes.

St. Patrick's Day Parade
Rue Ste-Catherine Consecutively since 1824, this

February: Festival Montréal en Lumière

©Jean-François Leblanc

MUST KNOW

popular parade reflects the Irish roots of the city and marks the end of winter.

April

Blue Metropolis – International Literary Festival

Various locations
(www.blue-met-bleu.com)
Brings writers and readers together across a wide spectrum of literary interests and languages.

Vues d'Afrique (African and Creole Film Festival)

Salle Gésu
(www.vuesdafrique.org)
The largest African film festival outside of the continent offers features, documentaries, and children's films celebrating the diaspora of cultures.

May

Festival TransAmériques (Theatre and Dance Festival of the Americas)

Various locations
(www.fta.qc.ca)
Multilingual hybrid festival bringing together original contemporary works reflecting the rhythms and voices of the surrounding community.

Montreal Bike Fest

Montreal streets and parks
(www.velo.qc.ca)
Montrealers from every quarter express their love of the bicycle in a festival covering the island with events around the clock.

June

First Peoples' Festival

Various locations
(www.nativelynx.qc.ca)
Ten days of festivities by First Nations Peoples from 3 Americas

June **F1 Grand Prix du Canada**

© Octane Management/Tourisme Montréal

and beyond, bringing together dance, music, theater, and food traditions.

Fringe Festival

Various theaters
(www.montrealfringe.ca)
Similar to a two-week block party, featuring the outrageous, experimental, and most nonsensical acts to be found.

F1 Grand Prix du Canada

Île Notre-Dame
(www.grandprixmontreal.com)
The single largest event on the city's yearly calendar attracts speed afficiandos and novices for a week of jetset excesses.

Mondial de la Bière (Beer Festival)

Various Locations
(www.festivalmondialbiere.qc.ca)
Free beer extravaganza features tastings, education, workshops, and contests for amateur and professional brew fans.

World Fireworks Competition

Île Ste-Hélène *(through Aug; www.international desfeuxloto-quebec.com)*
Spectacular waterside contest evokes joy throughout the city for travelers and locals alike.

July
Canada Day
Old Port *(www.celafete.ca)*
From noon until after midnight the Old Port celebrates Canada with cake, games, concerts, demonstrations, and fireworks.

Festival Juste Pour Rire
(Just For Laughs Festival)
Various locations
(www.hahaha.com)
World's premier laugh fest headlines with major names, unique acts, and an incredible free street party.

Festival International de Jazz de Montréal
Place des Arts area
(www.montrealjazzfest.com)
Guinness Books' *"Largest Jazz Festival in the World"* continues to amaze and delight public across all tastes with indoor concerts and free outdoor bonanza of sounds.

Festival International Nuits d'Afrique (African Nights)
Various locations
(www.festivalnuitsdafrique.com)

July: Festival Juste Pour Rire
©Juliane Martini/Michelin

From Timbuctu to Guadeloupe to North Africa and neighborhoods of Montreal, this compendium tribute to the sounds of Africa is constantly surprising and fun.

Osheaga Music & Arts Festival
Each July it feels like Woodstock has arrived at Jean Drapeau Park on Saint Helen's Island. Join in the fun for three days, on seven stages, with over 70 global acts.

August
Divers/Cité (Gay Pride)
Rues Berri & Ste-Catherine
(www.diverscite.org)
Award-winning GLBT festival lives up to its famous adage of being *"Mayhem of the highest order."*

La Fête des Enfants
(Children's Festival)
Park Jean Drapeau
(www.ville.montreal.qc.ca/fetedesenfants)
Diversity of fun lives here with a rich bounty of games, activities, crafts, music, and sports over two days.

Les FrancoFolies (French-language comedy and music)
Various locations
(www.francofolies.com)
The French language dominates

July: Festival International Nuits d'Afrique
©Denis Beaumont

MUST KNOW

proceedings here, but the world-class entertainment crosses barriers and delivers fun for all.

Montreal World Film Festival

Downtown cinemas
(www.ffm-montreal.org)
The international success of this festival relies upon the mandate of cultural diversity, innovation, independence, and creativity. Legions of film fans arrive here to savor the rich yearly program.

September

Marathon international de Montréal

(www.marathondemontreal.com)
Commencing on the Jacques-Cartier Bridge, this official Boston Marathon qualifying course is relatively flat and takes runners through neighborhoods like Old Port, Notre-Dame Island, etc.

Fall Festival-Orgue et couleurs
(Organ and colors)

Various locations
(www.orgueetcouleurs.com)
Classical organ concerts over 10 days present an international program celebrating the season of the changing colors of nature.

October

Black and Blue Festival
(Gay Celebration)

Various locations
(www.bbcm.org)
Started as a large private party, this week-long series of events has become one of the best gatherings to raise money for AIDS research and bring together the GLBT community from across Canada and around the world.

November

Coup de Coeur Francophone
(French-language music)

Various locations
(www.coupdecoeur.qc.ca)
French songs are the focus of this global festival, nurturing their introduction, cross-pollination, and recording.

Cinemania Film Festival

Cinéma Impérial
(www.cinemaniafilm festival.com)
Heralded as the "Leading French Film Festival in the Americas" for 10 days subtitles reign over an impressive cinematic itinerary.

December

Victorian Christmas

Sir George-Étienne Cartier National Historic Site
(www.pc.gc.ca/cartier)
From mid-November until Christmas relive the colorful festivities of a typical bourgeoise Montreal family of the 19C. Guides in period costume share the stories of the era, sit at the Victorian Christmas table, and immerse in the seasonal sights and sounds of entertaining unfold from another era.

December, Victorian Christmas, Sir George-Étienne Cartier National Historic Site

©Parks Canada

CALENDAR OF EVENTS

PRACTICAL INFORMATION

WHEN TO GO

Summer is the most popular season to visit Montreal. There are long hours of daylight, an intense schedule of free festivals, and only occasional spells of hot, humid weather. Late spring and early fall are also pleasant, with many outdoor activities still available. And the pleasures of a sunny Indian summer afternoon in October are not to be missed.

Then there is the special experience of a winter city, as Montreal moves indoors and underground for many of its daily activities, and outdoors for recreation, from skating rinks and cross-country ski trails to wintry celebrations. Sub-arctic chills are inevitable, but also brief, and there are thaws and even rain. In winter, facilities are uncrowded and room rates fall.

PLANNING YOUR TRIP

Before you go, contact Tourisme Québec, which handles inquiries from outside the city and will send information tailored to your request; or go to the Tourism Montreal website.

Tourisme Québec
1255 Rue Peel, bureau 400, Montreal, QC Canada H3B 4V4, *514-873-2015 or 877-266-5687.*
www.bonjourquebec.com

Tourisme Montréal
1255 Rue Peel Ste. 100, Montreal, QC Canada H3A 3L8
www.tourisme-montreal.org

Visitor Centers

Infotouriste Centre
1001 Rue du Square-Dorchester
Open year-round daily 9am–6pm; (Jun–Labour Day 9am–7pm)
Métro Peel, green line.

	Jan	Apr	Jul	Oct
Avg. High	-6°C / 21°F	11°C / 52°F	26°C / 79°F	13°C / 55°F
Avg. Low	-14°C / 7°F	1°C / 34°F	16°C / 61°F	5°C / 41°F

Average Seasonal Temperatures in Montreal
(recorded at Trudeau International Airport)

In the News

Find the most complete listings of films, theater, and exhibitions in English in the Saturday Weekend sections of **The Gazette**, available at all newsstands and online at *www.montrealgazette.com*. Free entertainment weeklies with extensive listings include **The Mirror** (www.montrealmirror.com) and **Hour** (www.hour.ca). These are often available at hotels and many Métro stations. Coverage is generally more detailed in the French-language media, including **La Presse** (www.cyberpresse.ca) and the more highbrow **Le Devoir** (www.ledevoir.com). The main free French-language weekly is **Voir** (www.voir.ca) and monthly **Fugues Magazine** covers GLBT lifestyle and community (www.fugues.com).

MUST KNOW

Important Phone Numbers	
Emergency (police/fire/ambulance, 24hr)	☏**911**
Info-Santé (24hr medical assistance)	☏811
Police (non-emergency)	☏514-280-2222
Community Health Centre and Medical Referral (CLSC)	☏514-934-0354
24-hour Pharmacy Pharmaprix, 5122 Côte-des-Neiges	☏514-738-8464
Weather	☏514-283-3010

Infotouriste Centre
174 Rue Notre-Dame Est, Old Montreal. *Open year-round daily 9am–5pm; (Jun–Labour Day to 7pm); Métro Place-d'Armes, orange line.*

Useful Passes
Unlimited **transit passes** are great value for intensive on-and-off bus and subway travel *(see Getting Around)*. The **Montreal Museums Pass** *(see Museums)* provides unlimited entry for three days, and an optional bargain transit pass.

GETTING THERE
By Air
Trudeau (Dorval) International Airport (YUL) is 14km/9mi from downtown *(514-394-7377 or 800-465-1213; www.admtl.com).* Taxis have fixed $38 fare to downtown. STM operates a 24/7 $8 bus to downtown called **747 Express** *(514-786-4636 option "0").* Regular coach buses operate to city center *(777 Rue de la Gauchetière Ouest)*, with shuttle connections to major hotels and to the Station Centrale d'Autobus at 505 Rue de Maisonneuve Est *(514-842-2281).*

By Train
Daily service to Montreal's **Central Station** *(Gare Centrale, Rue de la Gauchetière between Université*

Montreal Online
In addition to the tourism bureau sites shown, here are some websites to help you plan your trip:

+ www.ville.montreal.qc.ca
+ www.montrealinfo.com
+ www.vieux.montreal.qc.ca
+ www.canada.com/topics/travel/canada
+ www.montrealvisitors.com

& Mansfield) is provided by **VIA Rail** from major cities in Canada *(888-842-7245; www.viarail.ca)* and by **Amtrak** from New York City and Albany *(800-872-7245; www.amtrak.com).* **Commuter trains** serve suburbs on and off Montreal island from Central Station and from **Windsor Station** *(Rue de la Gauchetière at Peel).*

By Bus
Montreal's **Central Bus Station** *(Gare Centrale d'Autobus, 505 de Maisonneuve Est; 514-842-2281)* is the departure point for all buses. For travel from the US, contact **Greyhound** *(800-229-9424; www.greyhound.com)* or **Adirondack Trailways** *(www.trailwaysny.com; 800-858-8555).* For travel in the province of Quebec, contact

Bus and carriage, Old Montreal

©Richard Nowitz/Apa Publications

Orléans Express *(514-842-2281; www.orleansexpress.com).*
For travel from elsewhere in Canada, contact **Canadian Greyhound** *(www.greyhound.ca; 800-661-8747).*

By Car
Major expressways connect Montreal with New York City *(Autoroute 15 and I-87),* Boston *(I-89 and I-93),* and with Toronto and Quebec City. Bridges connect the island city with the mainland.

GETTING AROUND
The Street System
Most streets bear names, not numbers, and signs use French terminology *("rue"* for "street," usually dropped when giving an address, and *"est"* or *"ouest"* for east or west of Boulevard St-Laurent). On streets running roughly northward, buildings are numbered starting from the St. Lawrence River. Some street names have widely used informal English equivalents *(Rue de la Montagne/ Mountain Street).*

Car Rental		
Car Rental Company	✆**Reservations**	**Internet**
Alamo	800-327-9633	www.alamo.com
Avis	800-331-1212	www.avis.com
Budget	800-268-8900	www.budget.com
Dollar	800-800-4000	www.dollar.com
Enterprise	800-736-8222	www.enterprise.com
Hertz	800-263-0600	www.hertz.com
National	800-227-7368	www.nationalcar.com
Thrifty	800-847-4389	www.thrifty.com

MUST KNOW

By Car

No car is needed to get around the compact central area and in fact, it's best to avoid dealing with congestion, meters, and pay stations, confusing signs, and parking regulations. **Right turns on red lights are not permitted in Montreal**. Use of seat belts is required. Safety seats are required for children under 18kg/40lb; a booster seat is required for heavier children up to age eight. Drivers must yield to buses entering their lane from the right.

Lanes are reserved for taxis and buses on major streets during **rush hours** (7am–9am & 4.30pm–6.30pm). Some parking spaces are reserved for the handicapped, deliveries, and diplomats. Cars parked illegally may be ticketed, towed, or immobilized.

On Foot

Montreal is a compact city, with a central area only about 2km/1.24mi square and few challenging slopes. Walking is pleasant during most of the year. Ladies should refrain from high heels in the Old Port due to cobblestone streets.

In winter, icy sidewalks can be a hazard and appropriate clothing is a must. Underground passageways (see p 28) offer sheltered routes when it's cold or rainy, or humid outside. A map is handy to help you find your way and to locate passageways and

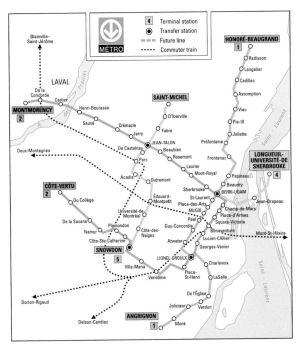

named streets. The free public transit map shows approximate street numbers.

Public Transportation

The **Societé des Transports de Montréal** *(514-786-4636; www.stm.info)* operates the island-wide subway and bus network. Free transfers are permitted between the two modes. Cash fare is $3.00, a strip of six tickets costs $14.25 *($8.50 for children under 12 and seniors 65+; children under age 5 ride free).* Unlimited passes are available to visitors April to October at most downtown Métro stations *(and at the Berri, Peel and Bonaventure stations all year)* for $8 *(one day)* and $16 *(three days; $65 with museum pass).*

The $22 weekly pass *(Sun–Sat)* available at any Métro station is the best value *($12.75 for youths & seniors).* Schedules are posted at many bus stops and can also be checked on the Internet.

Sherbrooke Métro station

©D. Reeve/Michelin

City Buses

Buses operate throughout downtown and the outer areas of the city. Use a pass or ticket, or pay a higher cash price. Remember, bus drivers don't make change. Most routes begin operation by 6am and end shortly after midnight. There are some rush-hour-only services and hourly service on a limited number of all-night routes.

Taxis

Taxis cruise Montreal streets or operate from taxi stands, charging $3.30 to start, $1.60 per km, or $0.60 per minute standing. Flat rates can be negotiated for long trips. There is no uniform taxi color; available cabs have an illuminated roof light. Major cab companies in Montreal include: **Atlas Taxi** *(514-485-8585);* **Diamond Taxi** *(514-273-6331);* and **Montreal Taxi Coop** *(514-725-9885).*

Subway

Montreal's subterranean commuter train system is the **Métro** and its arrow-in-a-circle logo, white on blue, prominently identifies stations. Two lines, the orange and the green, cross downtown from east to west, intersecting at either end of the central area. Métro trains operate from about 5.30am to 12.30am most days. Fares *($2.75)* are based on a flat rate. Buy subway tickets at station ticket booths or at convenience stores (called *dépanneurs*).

🚲 BIXI Bikes

This local bike rental service has 450 depots and a $5 per-day pricetag *(montreal.bixi.com).*

BIXI Bikes

© Tourisme Montréal

TIPS FOR SPECIAL VISITORS
Disabled Travelers

All museums and public buildings in Montreal have ramps and automatic doors for visitors in wheelchairs. Most major hotels provide accessible and adapted rooms. Disabled access is not required by law, however, so there are some exceptions.

Passengers travelling from the US who need assistance with train or bus travel should give advance notice to **Amtrak** *(800-872-7245 or www.amtrak.com)* or **Greyhound** *(800-752-4841/US, 800-661-8747/Canada, 800-345-3109/TDD; www.greyhound.com).* Request assistance when reserving on **VIA Rail** in Canada *(888-842-7245 or through any ticket office).* Wheelchairs may be reserved by calling the **Orléans Express** bus company *(800-419-8735).* Hand-controlled cars by reservation. Accessible **public transportation** on low-floor buses is provided on the main routes, only at stops displaying the universal accessibility symbol. Visitors

may also access the separate handicapped-only bus network; to arrange airport pickup, call *514-280-8211* before visiting. The subway *(Métro)* is **not** accessible to wheelchairs. Visitors can request an adapted van when phoning for a taxi.

Local Lowdown

The following organizations can provide detailed information about access for the disabled in the province of Quebec:

◆ **Kéroul**, an organization that promotes travel for the disabled, publishes *Québec accessible ($20; 514-252-3104; www.keroul.qc.ca).*

◆ The **Canadian government** provides information about accessible travel on its website: *www.accesstotravel.gc.ca/main-e.aspor. 1-800-665-6478.*

Senior Citizens

Many hotels, attractions, and restaurants offer discounts to visitors age 62 or older *(proof of age may be required)*. The **AARP** *(formerly the American*

Measurement Equivalents									
Degrees Fahrenheit	95°	86°	77°	68°	59°	50°	41°	32°	23°	14°
Degrees Celsius	35°	30°	25°	20°	15°	10°	5°	0°	-5°	-10°

Association of Retired Persons, 601 E St. NW, Washington, DC 20049; 202-434-7598; www. aarp.com) arranges discounts for its members, as does Canada's **Association for the Fifty-Plus** *(CARP, Suite 1304, 27 Queen St. E., Toronto, ON M5C 2M6; 416-363-7063; www.50plus.com).*

LANGUAGES

French is the official language of Quebec province and the majority language in Montreal. Businesses are generally required to use French in their operations and on signs. All road signs are in French. English is widely understood, especially downtown.

Glossary

In the *Must Sees* Montreal text, sight names are given in English and French, where applicable. Knowing a few words in Canadian French will come in handy:

yes – *oui*
no – *non*
exit – *sortie*
please – *s'il vous plaît*
thank you – *merci*
welcome – *bienvenue*
breakfast – *déjeuner*
lunch – *dîner*
dinner – *souper*
hello, good morning – *bonjour*
expressway – *autoroute*
goodbye – *bye*
gasoline – *essence*
how much? – *combien?*
collect call – *appel à frais virés*
where? – *où?*

subway – *Métro*
I don't understand –
  Je ne comprends pas
Do you speak English? –
  Parlez-vous anglais?

FOREIGN VISITORS

In addition to local tourism offices, visitors may obtain information from the nearest Canadian embassy or consulate in their country of residence. For further information on Canadian embassies, consult the website of the **Canadian Department of Foreign Affairs and International Trade:** *www.dfait-maeci.gc.ca.*

Area Codes

All of Montreal island uses the 514 and 438 area codes; the surrounding off-island suburbs use the 450 and 579 area codes. Include the area code *(without the long-distance "1" prefix)* when dialing all calls. Before you leave home, check with your carrier to make sure your cell phone will operate in Canada.
Montreal: 514 & 438
Off-island suburbs: 450 & 579
Quebec City: 418 & 581

Entry requirements

As of January 2007, citizens of the US need a valid passport or Air NEXUS card to visit Canada and return by air. A driver's license and a birth certificate together are currently accepted to enter Canada and return to the US by land or sea. Parents bringing children into Canada are strongly advised to carry birth certificates. As of 2008, only a passport or secure passport card will be accepted to return to the US. All other visitors to Canada must have a valid passport and, in some cases, a visa *(see list of countries at www.cic. gc.ca/english/visit/visas.asp).* No vaccinations are necessary. For entry into Canada via the US, all persons other than US citizens or legal residents are required to present a valid passport. Check with the Canadian embassy or consulate in your home country about entry regulations and proper travel documents.

Canada Customs

Visitors over 18 entering Quebec may bring 1.14 litres of liquor or 1.5 litres of wine or 24 x 12oz cans of beer without paying duty or taxes. Tobacco is limited to 200 cigarettes, 50 cigars, or 196g/7oz of loose product. Gifts totaling $60 Canadian may be brought in duty-free. All prescription drugs should be clearly labeled and for personal use only; carry a copy of the prescription. *(Check www.catsa. gc.ca for packing tips.)* Canada has stringent legislation on firearms—do not bring any weapons to the border *(for information, contact the Canadian Firearms Centre, Ottawa, Ontario K1A 1M6 Canada; 800-731-4000; www.cfc-ccaf.gc.ca).*

Money and Currency Exchange

United States currency is widely accepted, but it's best not to use it, given poor exchange rates. Currency exchanges are available at the airports, downtown *(along Ste-Catherine Street),* and at many banks. It's easiest to use credit cards for purchases or to withdraw money at a bank machine. Report lost or stolen credit cards to: **American Express** *(800-528-4800);* **Diners Club** *(800-234-6377);* **Master Card** *(800-307-7309);* or **Visa** *(800-336-8472).* Discover cards are not widely accepted in Canada. The **$** symbol in this book indicates Canadian currency. All prices shown are in Canadian dollars.

Driving in Canada

Drivers from the US may use valid state-issued licenses. Visitors from elsewhere should obtain an International Driving Permit through their national automobile association in order to rent a car. Drivers must carry a vehicle registration card or rental contract and proof of automobile insurance at all times. Gasoline is sold by the litre. Vehicles are driven on the right-hand side of the road.

Electricity

Voltage in Canada is 120 volts AC, 60 Hz, as in the US. Appliances from outside North America require adapters to Canadian voltage and flat-blade outlets.

Taxes

Generally, prices displayed in Canada do not include federal and provincial sales taxes *(totaling 13.5 percent in Quebec).* Sales tax applies to postage stamps, some food items, and many services.

Time Zone

Montreal is located in the Eastern Standard Time (EST) zone, five hours behind Greenwich Mean Time.

Tipping

Service charges are not included in restaurant prices. It's customary to give a small gift of money—a tip—for services rendered to waiters or taxi drivers *(up to 15% of fare)*, porters *($2 per bag)*, and chambermaids *($3 per day)*.

Weights and Measures

Canada is officially on the metric system. Gasoline is sold by the litre and produce by the kilo, while road distances are displayed in kilometres *(multiply by 0.6 for the approximate equivalent in miles)* and temperatures in degrees Celsius.

1 ounce	=	28 grams (gm)
1 mile	=	1.6 kilometres (km)
1 inch	=	2.54 centimetres (cm)
1 quart	=	0.94 litres
1 foot	=	30.48 centimetres
1 gallon	=	3.78 litres

ACCOMMODATION

For a list of suggested accommodations, see Hotels.

Reservation Services

www.Hotel de l'Institut 514-282-5120 *www.ithq.qc.ca/hotel.* **Downtown B&B Network** – 800-267-5180; *www.bbmontreal.qc.ca.* **Montreal Reservation B&B Network** – 800-917-0747;

Major hotel and motel chains with locations in or near Montreal include:

Property	✆ Phone	Website
Best Western	800-780-7234	www.bestwestern.com
Comfort, Clarion & Quality Inns	800-424-6423	www.choicehotels.com
Days Inn	800-329-7466	www.daysinn.com
Delta Hotels	877-814-7706	www.deltahotels.com
Fairmont	800-441-1414	www.fairmont.com
Hilton	800-445-8667	www.hilton.com
Holiday Inn	800-465-4329	www.holiday-inn.com
Hyatt	800-233-1234	www.hyatt.com
InterContinental	800-327-0200	www.ichotelsgroup.com
Marriott	800-228-9290	www.marriott.com
Méridien	800-543-4300	www.lemeridien.com
Omni	800-843-6664	www.omnihotels.com
Ramada Inns	800-272-6232	www.ramada.com
Ritz-Carlton	800-241-3333	www.ritzcarlton.com
Sheraton	800-325-3535	www.sheraton.com

Many hotels in all categories are listed on: www.tourisme-montreal.org. For a list of suggested lodgings, see Hotels.

MUST KNOW

Spectator Sports		
Sport/Team	Venue	✆Phone/Website
Montreal Canadiens		
Hockey Oct–Apr **(NHL)**	**Bell Centre**	Info: 514-790-1245 / 800-361-4595 www.canadiens.com
Montreal Alouettes		
Canadian June–Oct **Football** (Canadian Football League)	**Molson Stadium**	Info: 514-871-2255/ 514-790-1245 www.montrealalouettes.com
Montreal Impact		
Soccer Apr-Sept	**Claude-Robillard Stadium**	Info: 514-328-3668 www.montrealimpact.com

**www.montrealreservation.com.
Relais Montréal Hospitalité** –
*800-363-9635; www.martha-
pearson.com.*

Hostels
The **Montreal International
Youth Hostel** *(1030 Mackay;
514-843-3317; www.hostelling
montreal.com)* offers dormitory
beds for under $26 all year
to holders of the Hostelling
International card.

SPECTATOR SPORTS
Montreal is a great place to be
a spectator at sporting events.
Grand-Prix F1 car racing, the
single largest event of the year in
Montreal, brings spectators from
around the world for a week of fun
and frivolity in early June.
The streets bulge with visitors
and the pageantry, music, and
celebrations begin at noon
daily and continue well into the
following morning at clubs, bars,
and bistros throughout this special
week. The downtown **Bell Centre** is
home to the world's most winning
professional sports organization,
the Montreal Canadiens Hockey
Club.
This Mecca for hockey fans from
around the world is also located
one block from where professional
hockey first started, at the Victoria
Skating Rink in 1875.
The Montreal Alouettes Football
Club attracts another passionate
following at professional Canadian
Football League games held at
McGill University's recently
expanded Percival **Molson
Stadium**.
The newest sports attraction is
the Montreal Impact Professional
Soccer Team, holding exciting
matches at the newly constructed
Saputo Stadium *(Olympic
Stadium)*. Meanwhile, the annual
cycling race called Tour de l'Ile
reigns citywide around June
1st, Montreal Marathon in late
September, and legions of tennis
fans crowd the Roger's Cup
Competitions in July and August at
Uniprix Stadium *(Jarry Métro)*.

WELCOME TO MONTREAL & QUEBEC CITY

American-style efficiency, Canadian courtesy, Old World charm, the beauty of the French language in everyday life, Latin attitudes, and fabulous food: Circumstances, peoples, and geography have combined to make Montreal a metropolis like no other. It is a summer city with great gardens and parks, and a winter city that moves indoors and underground to overcome the climate, and outdoors to challenge it. It is a major port for the eastern half of the continent, and a high-tech capital; also a city hurtling into the future while confident in its traditions, where fashion and manners count as much as personal achievement.

MONTREAL – Montreal, peaceful and mannered today, grew out of conquests, colonization, and conflicts. This island in the St. Lawrence attracted the attention of French explorers, notably **Jacques Cartier**, who visited in 1535; **Samuel de Champlain**, who established a fur-trading outpost here in 1611, and **Paul de Chomedy**, Sieur de Maisonneuve, the founder of VilleMarie de Montréal in 1642.

Remote as it was, New France became involved in conflicts with England. Full-scale war erupted in 1756. The clifftop fortress at Quebec City gave way in 1759, and Montreal succumbed a year later. England now ruled North America, but it was only a change of management at the top. Under the **Quebec Act of 1774**, the Catholic religion was tolerated in Canada; and French civil law continued in effect. When the

Arrival of Champlain (1608) by George Agnew Reid

- Following annexations in 2002, Montreal covers most of an island measuring 50km by 30km (31mi by 18.6mi) where the Ottawa River joins the St. Lawrence.
- Two-thirds of Montrealers speak French as their first language.
- About 20 percent of the population of 1,600,000 (1,800,000 on the island) is foreign-born; many more are first-generation Québecois.
- The cross atop Mount Royal (Mont-Royal) is Montreal's signature, a monument to the missionaries and religious orders that shaped Quebec for much of its history.

American Revolutionary Army captured Montreal in 1775, the soldiers found a population largely unwilling to join its cause. Under the British, Montreal began to develop on the parallel tracks that have characterized the city to this day. French Canadians largely continued to cultivate the land or enter the priesthood or the law. In 1825, the **Lachine Canal** opened, bypassing rapids on the St. Lawrence River. Goods could now be landed in Montreal for shipment to the Great Lakes. Railroads and industry followed. Trains chugged in from the US over the Victoria Bridge in 1847 and by 1886, rails ran from Montreal to Vancouver.

Resentments simmered among the poorer French, who held no real political power. Rebellion broke out in 1837 and was quickly put down. Montreal became the capital of **United Canada**, but only until 1849, when rioters torched the parliament building on Place D'Youville. The city shrugged, and continued to grow, expanding its boundaries to take in neighboring villages. By the 20C, it had again become a largely French-speaking city. Some leaders even called for secession from Canada. Through the 20C, Montreal

became a leader in urban planning in cold climates. It rose upward and plunged underground into indoor commercial complexes and a state-of-the-art subway system; it dazzled the world as the host of a world's fair, **Expo '67**, and the **Olympic Games** in 1976.

Montreal has eventually taken stock, faced up to the challenges, mended its many strains, and continued to be . . . Montreal! The streets are safe and filled with strollers at all hours, even into the winter. International organizations and corporations take advantage of workers who speak more than one language; there's a moderate cost of living, a relaxed pace, excellent food, and a perfect mix of the familiar and the exotic. International companies continue to arrive here in record numbers, especially in the pharmaceutical, biotechnology, IT, media, and aviation industries. Construction projects once again dot the landscape, creating new urban landscapes and even altering neighborhood names, like **Quartier des Spectacles** (Entertainment District), **Cité des Arts du Cirque** (Cirque du Soleil's home), and **Cité Multi Media**. Two major new hospital mega-projects are underway, recharging the medical community with a much-needed surge of activity and inspiration. Downtown's Hopital Saint-Luc "super hospital" is being constructed near Old Montreal and will revitalize the central French health service core, while the larger **McGill University Health Centre** plan will amalgamate seven major hospitals into one new major West End location.

Ideally, visitors come to understand the up-close-and-personal aspect of Montreal life, but it's a good idea to first get an overview of this robust island-city. Go directly to the geographic highlight of the city, **Mount Royal.** Drive up the mountain from Park Avenue downtown to the Camillien-Houde Belvedere. It provides a dreamy viewpoint east over the city's working-class neighborhoods, the Olympic Tower, and the Saint Lawrence River. Further up Remembrance Road is the Mount Royal Chalet and the Kondiaronk Belvedere. From this lookout you can see downtown,

the South Shore, the Champlain, Victoria, and Mercier bridges, and the Monteregian mountains of Saint-Bruno, Saint-Hilaire, and Rougemont. Walk back along the trail to Maison Smith, home to Les Amis de la Montagne (Friends of the Mountain), a charitable organization passionately involved in nurturing the city's namesake. Other spots to view the city include the **Olympic Observatory**, world's highest inclined tower, Jean-Drapeau Park, extending across both **Saint Helen's** and **Notre-Dame Islands**, and Longueuil. Above all else, Montreal is a family city to explore and enjoy. The abundance of festivals serves up the latest world cultural performances, while the parks, stadiums, and outdoor activities supply a stream of adrenaline for all ages, and the late-night entertainment venues keep the party sizzling until the wee hours. Montreal's moment has arrived and obviously, it's a great time to visit.

QUEBEC CITY – Quebec City was at the creative apex of the term "New France" and unquestionably became the hub of all New World activity for those adventurers traveling from France over 400 years ago. On a regal outcropping high over the convergence of the **Saint-Lawrence and Charles rivers**, Quebec City, or "Kébec," as the Algonquin locals called it (meaning "where the river narrows") was a bustling Amerindian village of hunters and fishermen called Stadacona. Explorer **Jacques Cartier** arrived in 1535 and stayed long enough to name the promontory "Cap Diamant" (Cape Diamond) for King Francis I; it

Jacques Cartier by Théophile Hamel

Château Frontenac and Quebec City Old Town seen from the St. Lawrence River

©Tony Tremblay/iStockphoto.com

then became the largest military fortification in North America. On his second trip here, much later in 1608, fellow Frenchman **Samuel de Champlain** set up a fur trading post at Kébec. His team also crafted a wooden fort near the Notre-Dame-des-Victoires church, naming it "habitation."

The first real settlers did not arrive in Quebec City until the 17C. Location, location, location. Quebec City's longitude and latitude confirmed its position as the political, administrative, and military center of **New France**. Cape Diamond's 100m (300ft)-plus perch established a strategic military tool earning it the "Gibraltar of America" reputation. The British and French vollied ownership over many years, but only at the **Battle of the Plains of Abraham** leading to the Conquest of 1759 was there the **Treaty of Paris** in 1763, which made Quebec City, the former French colonial capital, capital of the **British** "Dominion." For two centuries Quebec City's

Old Port was the focal point for global trade. Fur led the menu of outgoing goods and the novelty of the shipping business as a whole gave birth to a building frenzy by the Brits here from 1820 until 1850. Quebec City experienced a short period of expansion in the 1920s. However, most jobs today are related to the seat of provincial government and the tourism service sector.

It is in **tourism** where Quebec City found a niche and with the beginnings of the preservation of the Old Town came international recognition. Now officially a UNESCO Heritage Site, visitors are able to unravel what life was like for these North American settlers. Today, the city welcomes travelers throughout the year across a wide variety of contemporary atttractions. A safe, clean, and upbeat locale, easily reached by air, road, rail, or water, the joie-de-vivre so famous in the Quebecers' character and lifestyle adds up to a highly desirable destination.

MONTREAL★★★

Located on the largest island of the **Hochelaga Archipelago** in the waters of the mighty St. Lawrence River, some 1,600km/1,000mi from the Atlantic Ocean, the cosmopolitan city of Montreal offers the visitor a wealth of attractions. Owing to its key position at the head of a vast inland waterway connecting the Great Lakes, the city is Canada's foremost port as well as a leading industrial, commercial, and cultural center.

The second-largest city in Canada after Toronto (which surpassed Montreal in the mid-1970s), Montreal is home to the world's largest Francophone population after that of Paris and displays a vibrant, distinctive French culture. The city's Anglophone community, concentrated primarily in the western part of the Island, also possesses a unique, interesting, blended character. Montreal has the distinction of being the Canadian urban center with the highest proportion of bilingual (English and French) and trilingual (usually English, French, and mother tongue of an immigrant) speakers. Old World cultures mesh in the North American setting and Nordic climate of Montreal, creating a fascinating vitality with an international flair. The city's numerous and varied ethnic groups sometimes make it seem like a miniature mosaic of the world.

GEOGRAPHY

Lying at the confluence of the Ottawa and St. Lawrence rivers, the island of Montreal measures 50km/31mi in length and 17km/10.5mi at its widest point. It is connected to the mainland by a tunnel and 15 road bridges, five of which span the St. Lawrence. Since 2006, the City of Montreal has been divided into 19 boroughs, occupying most of the Montreal Island, which is dominated by a 233m/764ft hill, known as Mont Royal. Nicknamed "the Mountain," Mount Royal is one of the Monteregian Hills, a series of eight peaks in the St. Lawrence valley.

VILLE SOUTERRAINE

Temperatures in Montreal change dramatically from season to season, but pedestrians can move throughout most of the business district without exposure to climactic extremes via "the underground city." Montreal's pedestrian city began in the 1960s with the construction of the landmark skyscraper, Place VilleMarie . Particularly remarkable for the spaciousness of its corridors and for its aesthetically "landscaped" atmosphere, the system connects the principal downtown hotels and office buildings, major department stores, hundreds of boutiques, several cinemas, numerous restaurants, two railway stations, the bus terminal, the city's major cultural center, Place des Arts; and two major convention centers, Place Bonaventure and Palais des Congrès. (In Quebec, the French word *place* commonly designates large interior spaces and commercial centers.)

NEIGHBORHOODS

Sure, there are ethnic enclaves like Chinatown, Little Italy, or Mile End, but Montreal's quartiers have twists you'll rarely find in North America. Travel back in time by strolling into Old Montreal, or explore public squares, or even unusual subterranean mazes. Find chic creations on Rue Saint-Denis and sleek fashions on Avenue Bernard in Outremont. You'll even encounter Westmount, where English-speakers are a quaint ethnic group with their own peculiar customs. Vive la différence!

OLD MONTREAL★★★
Vieux-Montréal

Stroll into the past in Old Montreal. Narrow cobblestone lanes (leave those high heels at the hotel), fieldstone colonial houses and convents, and early British commercial buildings were forsaken in the 19C as the business of Montreal, and its wealth, moved uphill. Today's business entrepreneurs have turned the once-forlorn area into an open-air museum of days gone by, with Montreal Science Centre, Pointe-à-Calliére Museum, & Bota-Bota Spa providing contemporary touches.

Place d'Armes★

Bounded by Rue St-Jacques, Rue Notre Dame, & Côte de la Place d'Armes. Métro Place-d'Armes, orange line.

Under the French regime, all authority radiated from this urban square, laid out more than 300 years ago, reputedly on the site where Paul de Chomedey, Sieur de (sire of) Maisonneuve, skirmished with a native chieftain.

A **statue [1]** *(see map on inside front cover)* of Maisonneuve and key figures from his day stands at the center.

To the south are the **Notre Dame Basilica★★★** *(see Landmarks)* and the **Old Sulpician Seminary★** *(see Historic Sites)*, seat of power for much of Montreal's history. On the north, the Bank of Montreal and the Royal Bank Building speak of the city's rising importance in the 19C and 20C.

Down nearby lanes and alleys you'll find meditation gardens, green oases in the city, still owned by the Church.

Old Montreal

NEIGHBORHOODS

Cruising the Neighborhoods: Boat Trips from the Old Port★

Since Montreal began as a riverside settlement and still thrives as a port, a boat trip is a must. Most cruises depart from the **Jacques Cartier Pier** at the Old Port *(Métro Champ-de-Mars, orange line)*.

- ♦ **Bâteau-Mouche** – *514-849-9952. www.bateaumouche.ca. May 15–Oct 15. Day cruise, $24 & up; dinner cruise $93–$150.* These Paris-style glassed-in "fly boats" ply the St. Lawrence River and islands.
- ♦ **AML Cruises** – *514-842-9300. www.croisieresaml.com. Departs from Old Port early-May–early-Oct. $28–$160.* AML operates sightseeing and dinner cruises; a river shuttle to Île Ste-Hélène or Longueuil *($7.00 one-way)*.
- ♦ **Amphi Tours** – Distinctive vehicle called the Amphibus boards clients for a unique ride through streets of Old Montreal, then directly into the water for a great view of the city. *514-849-5181. Métro Place d'Armes (www.montreal-amphibus-tours.com).*

Old City Walkabout

There's no better way to discover the charms of the old city than by following a whimsical course. Along the way, glimpse an old stone house in a courtyard through a coach entrance, find a shop full of surprises, or take a break at an inviting bistro. On the next page is a suggested walking route, or hire a *calèche* for a tour at a clip-clop pace *(see For Fun)*.

Rue Saint-Jacques★

Montreal's Wall Street is diminished from its heyday, but remains an important financial center. The **Bank of Montreal★** building on the north side of the Place d'Armes and the **Royal Bank of Canada★** are icons of the era of Montreal's financial ascendancy *(see Landmarks)*. The **Old Stock Exchange**, 453 Rue Saint-François-Xavier, a classical temple of a building, is now the **Centaur Theatre**. The new **Stock Exchange Tower★** *(Tour de la Bourse)* lies just to the west, at Victoria Square, across from the Montreal World Trade Centre.

Place Jacques-Cartier

Place Jacques-Cartier★★

Take wide, cobbled Place Jacques-Cartier from Rue Notre-Dame *(east of Place d'Armes)* down toward the port. What you see today dates from the heyday of English rule. The square's signature column is a **monument [2]** *(see map on inside front cover)* to Lord Horatio Nelson, victor of Trafalgar. Cafes and *terrasses* extend from sober stone buildings. Crowds and entertainers and flowers in bloom enliven the scene in mild weather. Just to the east are **Bonsecours Market★** *(see Must Shop)* and the **Chapel of Our Lady of Good Help★** *(see Historic Sites).*

Rue Saint-Paul★★

Head a block up from the Old Port and west along Rue Saint-Paul. Warehouses of old—mostly dating from the 19C—have been revived as boutiques and boutique hotels, ice cream shops, and fine restaurants, galleries, and clubs and of course, souvenir shops.

PLATEAU MONT-ROYAL★

East of Boul. St. Laurent.
Métro St-Laurent (green line) or
Sherbrooke (orange line).

To the east of Boulevard Saint-Laurent stretches Plateau Mont-Royal, a once-neglected neighborhood, where little brick

houses are just the right size for urban pioneers, who have spruced many of them up with bright paint, sanded floors, and modern wiring.

Boulevard Saint-Laurent

From the Old Port north.
Métro St-Laurent (green line) or
Sherbrooke (orange line).

Locally known as The Main (as in Main Street), Boulevard Saint-Laurent is the traditional dividing line between French and English Montreal, where waves of immigrants first stopped. Landmarks include **Schwartz's Deli** *(3895 Boul. St-Laurent; see Restaurants),* famous world-wide for Montreal smoked meat. As on upper Saint-Denis, low rents and large spaces have attracted entrepreneurs to former clothing factories and warehouses. At all hours, The Main is alive with trendy bars (frequented by students from McGill University

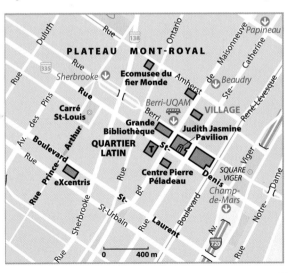

Princely Lunch on a Pauper's Purse

The competition is fierce among the Greek restaurants along lively Rue Prince-Arthur, to everyone's benefit. 🔥 **Mazurka (64 Rue Prince Arthur, 514-844-3539)** features homecooked Polish fare, and is just one of numerous establishments that offer a soup-to-dessert meal for less than $12 at lunch and most evenings. Without a doubt the best soups in the city, plus pierogis, potato latke, and schnitzel to remember. The quality and quantity of food, considering the price, is surprising. And that's not all—most of the Rue Prince-Arthur establishments allow you to bring your own bottle of wine, which the waiter will uncork and serve at no additional charge. Stop in at the SAQ (liquor store) around the corner on Boulevard St-Laurent **(corner of Pine Avenue)** before you dine. Menus are posted at most restaurants in the city.

to the west and UQAM to the east), and if there's a cuisine in the world that might find a local following, chances are it's available somewhere on this street. As a shopping destination, The Main is a happy mix of upscale and downscale, with plenty of bargains still available in its unpretentious shops. **Ex-Centris cinema complex** – *3536 St-Laurent. See Performing Arts.*

Rue Prince-Arthur

Turn east from Saint-Laurent onto Rue Prince-Arthur, named for a former governor-general and son of Queen Victoria. You're now on a one-time street of immigrants gone countercultural in the 1960s and a little bit glitzy in the present. The asphalt has been lifted in favor of paving blocks and pedestrians have the run of the former road, along with street performers, sidewalk artists, and patrons of the sidewalk tables that overflow from restaurants up and down the way—where the cuisine of Greece prevails. By night, it's even busier as patrons flow in and out of bars, most especially the venerable **Café Campus** *(57 Rue Prince-Arthur Est).*

Carré St-Louis★

Continuing eastward, Rue Prince-Arthur is suddenly sedate as it ends at **St. Louis Square**, a garden with towering trees and a pavilion-cum-creperie-cum market, plus water fountain at its center, surrounded by substantial 19C town houses with ornate detailing and decorative roofs. The greats of French-Canadian arts made their homes here, including poet Émile Nelligan, and secessionist sentiment is sometimes expressed through the display of the provincial flag. Take a break on a park bench for some of the local color before continuing eastward to Rue Saint-Denis (see p 34). There's a charming farmers' market attached to the créperie, too.

THE OLD PORT★
Le Vieux-Port

Rue de la Commune centered at Boul. St-Laurent. 514-496-7678. www.quaysoftheoldport.com. Métro Place-d'Armes or Champ-de-Mars, orange line.

Down at the base of Place Jacques-Cartier, cross waterside Rue de la Commune, enter the garden, and look toward the river and the piers of the Old Port. For centuries, canoes and ocean-going ships made it to this point on the St. Lawrence and no farther, stopped by rapids just around the bend. A few blocks toward the west is the restored entry to the Lachine Canal, which bypassed the rapids in 1825 and helped to make Montreal the second-busiest port on the continent. Now, take a look behind. To the left and right spread buildings hardly changed in one hundred years, two-, three- and four-stories tall, some clad in stone, others showing iron frames. Perhaps not a single one is architecturally "distinguished," but as a group, they bring a slice of an 18C port into the present day. Faded signs in English and French announce supply services; archways lead to former stables.

Port Revived – Cross the rail tracks *(mostly unused)* at any of a number of points into Montreal's Old Port itself, stretching 2.5km/1.5mi along the waterfront. Join the crowds on the great **esplanade** to enjoy the season, by motorized **tram**, rented bicycle, in-line skates, pedal boat, or ice skates. Attractions include the **Montreal Science Centre★** with its IMAX theater, on King Edward Pier *(see For Kids)*. Take a cruise *(see p 35)*, or climb the **Clock Tower** (Tour de l'Horloge),

Look Out Below!

Roofs on homes in the Old Port and other areas are steeply pitched, in the absence of interior drains, to shed snow to the street below. If you're out in a dreamy winter cityscape after a heavy fall, watch out!

erected in 1922 in memory of merchant sailors.

RUE SAINT-DENIS★ AND THE LATIN QUARTER
Quartier Latin

Rue St-Denis between Rue Ste-Catherine & Rue Sherbrooke. www.quartierlatin.ca. Métro Berri-UQAM or Sherbrooke, orange line.

If Montreal's heart is at Place d'Armes, its French soul is in the Quartier Latin, along Rue Saint-Denis. Theatrers, art-movie houses, and bookstores express the latest in *Québécois* culture. Cafes are thronged at all hours, in every season.
The Université de Québec à Montréal (UQAM) and the National Library of Quebec were established here to preserve and protect a language and culture perceived as imperiled in a continental sea of English—hence the nickname (as in the Latin Quarter area of Paris near La Sorbonne). Names,

© AllCanadaPhotos/Photoshot

Rue Saint Denis

NEIGHBORHOODS

faces, and buildings have changed, but the Latin Quarter remains a cultural capital of Quebec. The new Grande Bibliothéque on Rue Berri *(corner of Rue de Maisonneuve)* has established this zone as one for all cultures and Montrealers flock here in astounding numbers.

Rue Saint-Denis★

Stroll the *rue* and check out the myriad restaurants and boutiques, but there are sights to note as well. The **Université de Québec à Montréal** (UQAM) occupies modern and heritage buildings along Saint-Denis *(south of Rue Ste-Catherine).* **Théâtre St-Denis** [**T**] *(see map p 36)* showcases French-language singers, including Céline Dion.

Farther North – Above Rue Sherbrooke, and stretching onto side streets as far as Rue Duluth, lies the more avant-garde sector of St-Denis, where the studios, restaurants, and boutiques of Quebec's up-and-coming fashion designers, chefs, jewelers, bakers, and even soap-makers crowd the wide sidewalks.

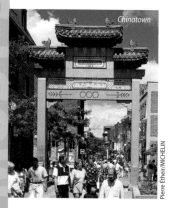

Chinatown

Pierre Ethier/MICHELIN

CHINATOWN★

Rue de la Gauchetière between Rue Côté & Boul. St-Laurent. Métro Place d'Armes and Saint-Laurent.

You'll find all the elements of a North American Chinese quarter along pedestrians-only Rue de la Gauchetière, and in the blocks to the north and south: herbal shops, inexpensive wares from the People's Republic, exquisite lacquerware, pressed duck ready for carryout, a fortune-cookie factory, a Holiday Inn with a pagoda roof, and restaurants, restaurants, restaurants! Montreal's Chinatown emerged in the 1860s after railroad construction workers and mine laborers resettled in cities wherever the rails ran. In time, like other immigrants, the Chinese moved on into the larger society, but successive waves of immigrants have maintained the character of Montreal's Chinese quarter.

What To Do In Chinatown

Every excursion to Chinatown begins with a walk along **Rue de la Gauchetière**. Branch out to the busy intersecting streets lined with merchants, especially Boulevard St-Laurent and Rue Clark. The little park at la Gauchetière and Clark honors Sun Yat-Sen, first president of the Chinese Republic. The site of the first-hand laundry, at St-Antoine and Jeanne-Mance, is something of a local landmark. The Holy Spirit Catholic Mission at 205 Rue de la Gauchetière features a unique series of Oriental paintings of the Stations of the Cross, while the church is a designated historic landmark.

OUTREMONT

On the eastern flank of Mont-Royal, west of Ave. du Parc and north of Boul. Mont-Royal. From Métro Laurier on the orange line it's a nice walk or Outremont on the blue line places you at the core.

What Westmount is to traditional English Montreal, Outremont is to French Montreal: well-off, well-educated, substantially constructed early in the 20C. Lawyers, doctors, politicians, and teachers reside in Second Empire houses, though they only scale the lower reaches of the mountain.

Avenue Laurier

Outremontais (residents of Outremont) have their equivalent of Westmount's Greene Avenue, but Avenue Laurier offers a more varied selection of clothing boutiques, *pâtisseries*, cheese shops, and restaurants proposing refined cuisine. On Greene Avenue, a couple of restaurants set out chairs and tables in mild weather; in Outremont, the sidewalk cafes look as if they belong.

Avenue Bernard

The other main shopping street of Outremont, Avenue Bernard, is livelier and more avant-garde in its restaurants and boutiques. Dine at **Nonya** *(151 Rue Bernard, 514-875-9998)* for authentic Indonesian cuisine, and dessert at **Glacier Le Bilboquet** *(at no. 1311)*, serving its fabled ice cream in warm weather and cold. Restaurants here are known for sleek decor and arresting presentation, as well as good food.

WESTMOUNT

North and South of Rue Sherbrooke. Métro Atwater (green line) on the east extremity and Métro Vendome (orange line) on the west, or bus 24 Sherbrooke St.

"English" in Montreal refers to anyone who speaks the language, regardless of background ("*anglophone*," more accurately, in French), but the district of Westmount, for many years a separate municipality with its own quirky ways, comes as close as you'll find to England itself.

More of Westmount

For more English-Canadian flavor, continue westward along Sherbrooke a couple of blocks to the lawn bowling green at the Old City Hall grounds, where you'll see players garbed in whites from April onward. Farther West, at Sherbrooke and Melville, sits **Westmount Park**, with its updated centenary library and oh-so-English greenhouse.

QUARTIER DES SPECTACLES★★

www.quartierdesspectacles.com

The Entertainment District, or Quartier des Spectacles, is the biggest new change to the core of Montreal's urban landscape. Comprising one tiny square kilometre (including the legendary "Red Light District"), this is home to 6,000 residents, but you will discover 80 indoor and outdoor cultural venues featuring over 28,000 seats, including 30 performance halls, manned by 7,000 cultural employees, attracting over 5,000,000 festival

NEIGHBORHOODS

35

attendees yearly. This dynamo cultural quadrant begins at Rue Sainte-Catherine and Boulevard Saint-Laurent, and extends from Rue City Councillors to Rue Saint-Hubert, Rue Sherbrooke, and Boulevard Rene Levesque. Note the exciting new Montreal Symphony Hall directly adjacent to Place des Arts.

CITÉ DU MULTIMEDIA

A new neighborhood designation comprising the area west of McGill Street *(Old Montreal)* between Griffintown and downtown's Bonaventure Expressway. Old refurbished warehouses occupied by high-tech companies mix with renovated centuries-old residences and new high-rise condos, creating a unique huddle near the waterfront. Once a seemingly abandoned area of light-manufacturer's brick buildings, the streets are alive around the clock now, as the multimedia community works, plays, and sleeps here.

CITÉ DES ARTS DU CIRQUE

www.tohu.ca

One of the world's largest circus arts creation, training, distribution, and production centers. Partly financed by Cirque du Soleil *(global HQ is here)*, this zone's mandate is multi-tiered. Initially constructed to promote Montreal as a world center for the circus arts, it has become a major neighborhood reinvention concept, successfully rehabilitating the Saint-Michel Environmental Complex *(182ha/450 acres of landfilled quarry)*. Circus arts productions are performed

in the round by an international list of creators, with the entire development being one of the most amazing green architecture examples anywhere.

Many free shows are scheduled each month, as well as performance workshops, circus history exhibitions, environmental events, and conferences *(2345 Rue Jarry, east; Métro Jarry + 193 bus; 514-376-8648)*.

QUARTIER INTERNATIONALE

www.qimtl.qc.ca

Quartier Internationale covers the area from University east to include the Bell Tower, ICAO (UN), Place Victoria, Stock Exchange Tower, W Hotel, Place Jean-Paul Riopelle, InterContinental Hotel, the newly renovated Palais des congrés (convention center), plus assorted condo projects either refurbishing buildings, or housed in contemporary structures.

The overall effect is liveable urban chic. Diners wishing to try the legendary French eatery Toqué will find it fronting Place Riopelle. Don't be surprised to see Riopelle's bronze sculpture-fountain La Joute (Joust) ablaze with rings of fire each evening starting at 6.30pm. It is quite a sight as the reflections bounce off multi-colored windows across the street.

All major sites in this quartier are connected underground to the Métro subway system and the famous Underground City, over 20 miles/32 km of tunnels, hallways, shopping options, and curios. This network is a great option to keep for a bad weather day.

HISTORIC SITES

With almost 400 years behind the city since the French settled, and a people as proud of their past as their present, Montreal packs a historical punch hard to equal on this side of the ocean. Turn a corner downtown, and you'll come across a church filled with hymns for centuries; a humble stone residence with a steep roof that has shed snow through hundreds of winters, the town home where a bourgeois family dwelled before there were fashionable suburbs, or a quiet, ecclesiastical garden now surrounded by skyscrapers.

BONSECOURS MARKET★
Marché Bonsecours

350 Rue St-Paul Est, along the waterfront. 514-872-7730. www.marchebonsecours.qc.ca. Open Jun 27–Sep 7 daily, 10am–9pm; check website for other seasonal times of operation. Exhibition hall hours vary. Métro Champ-de-Mars, orange line.

Bonsecours Market

© zimmytws/Bigstockphoto.com

Standing above the rooftops of **Old Montreal★★★**, the central silvery dome of Bonsecours Market bespeaks power and purpose well beyond its function as a humble market. When viewed from the water, the cut-stone facade, with its oversized windows and columned portico, is as grand as any palace in Venice. Bonsecours has indeed been more than a market. It began as a place for the exchange of goods in 1847, replacing the outdoor markets subject to inclement weather on Place Jacques-Cartier.

The plan of builder William Footner was to impress all with

Maison du Calvet★

405 Rue Bonsecours. 514-282-1725. www.pierreducalvet.ca. Métro Champ-de-Mars, orange line. One of the more notable homes that remains from the French **régime** once belonged to Pierre du Calvet. A noncomformist in every way, he was a merchant in a colony of priests and farmers, a Protestant among Catholics, a supporter of the British against the French, and later of the revolutionary Americans against the British. His residence was erected in 1725 at the northeast corner of the intersection of Rue St-Paul with Rue Bonsecours. The house of Pierre du Calvet now shines as an elegant hotel, with romantic dining at its Filles du Roy restaurant, or drinks in the Greenhouse, or by the fire in their plush Library.

HISTORIC SITES

the "overwhelming image of the beauty and importance of the flourishing City of Montreal." Over the years, the Greek Revival-style building morphed into Montreal's city hall, a concert auditorium, and for a time became the seat of the Parliament of United Canada after the legislature on Place d'Youville was torched in the rioting of 1849.

It also remained the city's premier farmers' market until 1963. With its former grandeur now restored, the structure comprises a collection of upscale boutiques, specialty shops, and eateries lining the interior (see Shopping).

CHÂTEAU RAMEZAY★

280 Rue Notre-Dame Est. 514-861-3708. www.chateauramezay.qc.ca. Open Jun–Oct daily 10am–6pm; Oct–May Tue–Sun 10am–4.30pm. $10, $8 seniors, $7 students, $5 youths over 5 years. Métro Champ-de-Mars, orange line.

Though far from the *métropole* of Paris, the administrators of New France made few concessions to their wild surroundings. You can see it in Governor Claude de Ramezay's mansion, completed in 1705. While other buildings huddled along narrow lanes, the Governor's great stone residence stood on an expansive estate. The new British overlords took over the premises after the Conquest (known in French to this day as *La Défaite*, The Defeat). Invading American Revolutionaries set up headquarters here in 1775 and Benjamin Franklin was offered the entertainments of the house. Château Ramezay was expanded over the years and remodeled to create huge, vaulted spaces. The original kitchens and service areas remain.

An oddity is the antique mahogany paneling in the Salle de Nantes, which found its way here in the 20C. It originally graced the headquarters of the French West India Company, which once owned the property.

Museum – Pieces on display—Native artifacts, clothing, letters, tools—illustrate life on Montreal island, when survival of the community depended on the goodwill of Amerindians, unsteady supply lines, and adaptation to an unforgiving winter *(visit onsite*

Château Ramezay, Historic Site and Museum of Montréal

boutique for AmerIndian gifts). Be sure to see the collection of early Canadian paintings from the 18C and 19C. Recorded music and personnel in period costumes help to recreate entertainment among the highbrow, and the daily round of chores for those who served them.

Cafe and Gardens – You'll be as privileged as the governor of yore to avail yourself of his gardens in mild weather, with the additional amenity of a contemporary cafe. This replanting is practical as well as attractive. It includes a kitchen garden *(potagerie)* and orchard, as well as plants for decoration and a border of herbs and medicinal plants. Entry to the gardens is free.

MARGUERITE BOURGEOYS MUSEUM★

Notre-Dame-de-Bon-Secours Chapel

400 Rue St-Paul Est. 514-282-8670. www.marguerite-bourgeoys.com. Open May–Oct Tue–Sun 10am–5.30pm, Nov–mid-Jan & Mar–Apr Tue–Sun 11am–3.30pm. Closed mid-Jan–Feb. $10 (free entry to chapel). Métro Champ-de-Mars, orange line.

Montrealers are fond of Bon-Secours Chapel. Because it's the church of the much-loved Sister Marguerite Bourgeoys and the favorite chapel of sailors, moves to demolish the church have always been defeated. The current Bon-Secours Chapel was constructed starting in 1771, directly over the foundations of the first stone church in Montreal. It has the typically tall steeple of a country church, sheathed in copper. Inside, Bon-Secours radiates humility. Its notable decorations are not gilt altarpieces, but late-19C paintings on fitted boards of wood. Carved ships, gifts from sailors, hang in the sanctuary.

Museum – Marguerite Bourgeoys (1620–1700) founded the original church and school on the site. Born into prosperity, she gave up her worldly advantages to become the first teacher on the island. She established the Congregation of Notre Dame, the first order of nuns in the Americas to minister to the community outside the cloister. Former classrooms and parts of the tower make up the museum devoted to her works and memory. Her story is partly told through doll-like figures in a series of vignettes. Marguerite was elevated

---

Above and Below

While you're exploring the church, climb the stairway to the tower, completed in 1894 as the base of the 9m/30ft statue of the Virgin Mary with arms outstretched toward the river. The upper terrace offers one of the best and highest **panoramas★** of Old Montreal, and of the St. Lawrence River and its islands. Then descend below the nave and back in time. Excavations have revealed the foundations of the original stone church, wooden posts from colonial fortifications, charred remains from the 1754 fire that destroyed the original church, and signs of an aboriginal settlement, perhaps more than 2,000 years old.

HISTORIC SITES

to sainthood in 1982 and the order continues to operate the attached mission for the indigent.

THE OLD FORT AND STEWART MUSEUM★

20 Chemin Tour-de-l'Île, Île Ste-Hélène. 514-861-6701. www.stewart-museum.org. Open year-round mid-May–mid-Oct daily 10am–5pm. Rest of the year Wed–Mon 10am–5pm. Closed Jan 1 & Dec 25. $10. Métro Jean-Drapeau, yellow line, then bus 167.

Old Fort *(Vieux-Fort)* – British authorities decided to fortify Montreal, and with good reason. The rebellious Americans had occupied the city in 1775 and the young nation had invaded Canada in 1812. The colonial government acquired St. Helen's Island in 1818 and began construction of defenses. Eventually, the American threat eased and the fort was abandoned.

Stewart Museum★ *(Musée David M. Stewart)* – Completely renovated in 2011 and located in the Old Fort, this museum was founded in 1955 by philanthropist David M. Stewart (1920–84), heir to the MacDonald Tobacco fortune. Exhibits tell the story of the two European powers, their North America clashes and campaigns in Canada, from the American invasions of 1775 and 1812 to the *Patriote* rebellion of 1837 and expeditions to the Pacific. There are weapons, maritime instruments, maps and documents, to be sure, and complete military uniforms from early in the 19C, as well as all the utensils and instruments used to prepare food and to light dwellings.

OLD SULPICIAN SEMINARY★

Vieux Séminaire de Saint-Sulpice

130 Rue Notre-Dame Ouest. Métro Place d'Armes, orange line.

On Place d'Armes next to the **Notre Dame Basilica★★★** *(see Landmarks)*, the Vieux Séminaire is the oldest building standing on the island of Montreal. It was completed for the Sulpician order in 1687, when running a religious brotherhood meant a lot more than serving God.

The Order – Founded in Paris by Jean-Jacques Olier in 1641, the Sulpician Order was firmly rooted in Montreal by the mid-17C. The Sulpicians acquired the mission of VilleMarie in 1663—a sort of franchise that made them feudal masters of the island of Montreal for more than 200 years, entrusted by the King with maintaining the good order of his properties and of the people who occupied them.

The Seminary – The Sulpicians were already well established in New France by the time construction started on their seminary. Of course as secular powers, they sited their base of operations on Place d'Armes, the very center of authority. Rough stonework, dormers, and the relatively steep roof to shed snow are characteristic of early Quebec buildings that take advantage of local materials, but this is a classical building in local garb. The pediments, inset columns, and orientation around an open courtyard—not the best solution for Montreal's chilly climate—were transplanted directly from France. The premises expanded with

History Lives

The power of the Old Fort's tale lies in the telling. Throughout the summer, troops of the Olde 78th Fraser Highlanders and the Compagnie franche de la Marine drill and prepare for battle, while keeping a wary eye on each other. The Highlanders, in Tartan kilts, break the monotony of garrison duty with dances performed to the skirl of bagpipes. Maneuvers take place daily at 11am, parades at 3 and 4.30pm. The 1pm salute by the 24-pounder Bloomfield gun can be heard on Mount Royal. *Reenactments are held daily late-Jun–late-Aug. Call or check online for latest schedules.*

the order; the main building was enlarged in 1704 and 1712, and the courtyard wings added.

Today the building continues to serve as a residence for the Sulpician Order.

Seminary Clock – Set into the seminary roof, the clock dates from 1701, which makes it one of the oldest anywhere in the United States and Canada. Oddly, its wooden mechanism survived until 1966, when it was replaced with modern electrical workings.

SIR GEORGE-ÉTIENNE CARTIER NATIONAL HISTORIC SITE★

Lieu Historique National du Canada de Sir George-Étienne Cartier

458 Rue Notre-Dame Est. 514-283-2282. www.pc.gc.ca/cartier. Open late-May–Aug daily 10am–6pm. Apr–late-May & Sept–late-Dec Wed–Sun 10am–noon & 1pm–5pm. Closed Jan–Mar. $4 ($6 with seasonal reenactments, call or consult website for schedule). Métro Champ-de-Mars, orange line, or bus 14.

If any man embodies the struggle to make Canada, it's George-Étienne Cartier. Born in a small town in 1814, he started his public life by taking up arms and had to flee after the failed 1837 Patriote rebellion. But back he came to achieve by peaceful methods what he couldn't accomplish with a gun: representative government with a place for French Canadians, both in their home region and in Ottawa. The ex-rebel ended up Sir George-Étienne, knighted by Queen Victoria. He helped establish the spirit of compromise and tolerance that would come to characterize political dialogue in Canada. Today he is venerated as a civil hero, one of the Fathers of Confederation.

The Buildings – The Cartier property consists of two adjoining homes used by the family in different periods. On the street side they're built in an early version of the Second Empire style, with gables and pitched sections of roof at the top, and imposing cut-stone facing. Yet the rear exposure, in rough fieldstone, is deeply rooted in traditional Quebec. The buildings and rooms have been restored to recreate the days when Cartier lived here.

HISTORIC SITES IN THE 21C

What to do with a convent that's no longer in use but occupies valuable property? A heritage church that has lost its congregation? A stately

Life and Times of Sir George-Étienne

Reenactments at the Sir George-Étienne Cartier NHS highlight the lives of the famous and the less so in the times of Cartier. Have a taste of the old art of fine living, when the leisure class made its own entertainment using the piano in the salon, and servants (all apparently still in the employ of the house, in this case) scurried about to please owner and guests. The interiors are the height of refined elegance of the time, with gold-leaf molding and plush wallpaper. Sound effects, from a steam engine to church bells, echo the street music of the day. Oversized photos reproduce downtown scenes and mannequins display Victorian outfits. Upstairs, the focus is on Cartier (1814–73), first as a lawyer and businessman, and later, as cabinet minister.

hotel long on charm but short on modern amenities?

Why knock it down when you can stabilize it, clean it, re-wire it, and build a new building under and around it while preserving the beauty of times gone by and contributing to the ambience of the city? Not to mention making a profit. In Montreal, what goes up doesn't have to come down.

It's part of living in the present with grace and traditions that elsewhere are in the past.

Here are some examples:

Christ Church Cathedral★

1444 Ave. Union at Rue Ste-Catherine. 514-843-6577. www.montrealcathedral.ca. Open year-round daily 10am–5pm & for services. Métro McGill, green line.

On the surface, Christ Church Cathedral appears much as it always has. The landmark Anglican church of Montreal, designed by Frank Wills and built of limestone, was completed in 1859 to serve the elite of its day, but a declining congregation led to financial straits. In addition, the church was literally sinking. The solution was to lease the land to the north of, and *under* the landmark for commercial development.

For several years, the cathedral sat perched in the air on concrete piers while the **Promenades de la Cathédrale** shopping complex was excavated beneath and the office tower now known as **Tour KPMG★** was erected to the north, mirroring the church in its polished aluminum surface, cavernous lobby, and peaked roof.

The neo-Gothic cathedral is now as glorious as ever, famed for its organ and choirs. Note the carved stone above the arches, depicting the foliage of Mount Royal.

The Coventry Cross is made of nails from the bombed-out cathedral in Coventry, England, and the stone screen behind the altar is a World War I memorial, engraved with scenes from the life of Jesus.

If you're not familiar with the spire, you'll do a double take. No, it's not stone, at least not any more! The weighty 1927 original, added to inadequate underpinnings, caused the whole church to sink.

It was replaced in 1940 with this faux-stone spire made of lightweight aluminum.

Maison Alcan★

1188 Rue Sherbrooke Ouest.
Open year-round daily, 7am–
midnight. Métro Peel, green line.

Can a modern aluminum
skyscraper co-exist with a hotel
that has seen better days? In the
same neighborhood? On the same
site? Evidently so, for Maison Alcan
was the company's showcase
before their recent move to larger
digs. Both as a company using a
beautiful building material, but also
one in harmony with the former
hotel and adjacent town homes
it envelops, Alcan led the pack
with this concept.
Daring in its use at the time
(1983), aluminum has become
the sheathing of choice in
modern, energy-saving buildings
in Montreal, covering layers of
insulation and mimicking windows
where there are none.
Along similar lines is the **Banque
Nationale de Paris★ (BNP)**,
a few blocks away on Avenue
McGill College near Sherbrooke,
which envelops a row of elegant
greystone town houses that would
otherwise have been demolished.

Le Windsor★

1170 Rue Peel. Métro Peel,
green line.

The elegant Windsor Hotel of
1878 lost its main wing to fire
in 1957, and the CIBC Tower went
up on the site. Until 1981 the hotel
functioned in what remained—an
outsized mansion with a huge
mansard roof relieved by dormers
and rounded windows.
It lives once again in the restored
splendor of suites occupied
by today's business giants.

Unfortunately, the ornate interior
atrium is not open to the public.

Dawson College

3040 Rue Sherbrooke Ouest.
www.dawsoncollege.qc.ca.
Open year-round Mon–Sat.
Closed Sun & school holidays.
Métro Atwater, green line.
514-931-8731.

Former Mother House of the
Congregation of Notre Dame,
Dawson College occupied a prime
piece of underutilized real estate
on the western edge of downtown.
The facilities of a junior college
were scattered in several buildings
in an industrial area down the hill.
In 1998, after extensive renovation,
the two were joined, with new
facilities built largely into the
ground.

Judith Jasmin Pavilion, Université de Québec à Montréal

405 Rue Ste-Catherine Est at Berri.
Métro Berri-UQAM.

The entire Saint Jacques Church
was not saved when the University
of Quebec expanded its Montreal
downtown campus between 1976
and 1979, but the lovely Gothic
facade on Rue Berri was salvaged,
along with the bell tower and
transept. The abbreviated church
is further reflected in the arched
passageways of the new building.
The popular **Galerie UQAM**
operates a contemporary art
gallery showcasing modern
works from Quebec, Canada,
and around the world.

HISTORIC SITES

LANDMARKS

Landmark or historic site? Given Montreal's rich past, the lines sometimes blur, but there are plenty of tours de force in Montreal's urban fabric, both old and new.

NOTRE DAME BASILICA★★★
Basilique Notre-Dame

110 Rue Notre-Dame Ouest. 514-842-2925. www.basiliquenddm.org. $5. Open Mon–Fri 8am–4.30pm, Sat 8am–4.00pm, Sun 12.30pm–4.00pm. Métro Place d'Armes, orange line, or the 55 city stops east of basilica.

Notre Dame is where celebrities mark their milestones, whether they attend Mass or not regularly. Pop diva Céline Dion was married inside. Pierre Elliott Trudeau's funeral ended with a rendition of "**O Canada**" on the carillon as an honor guard of Mounties bore his casket down the steps (while Jimmy Carter chatted with Fidel Castro). On both joyful and

Sound and Light
Et la lumière fut (And There Was Light) celebrates Montreal's history and heritage with lights, sound effects, and screens, drapes, and scenery that magically disappear after each performance. Altogether, it's a high-tech event in a traditional setting. *Tue–Thu 6.30pm, Fri 6.30 & 8.30pm, Sat 7 & 8.30pm, also Tue–Thu 8.30pm in summer; tickets are $10 at the Basilica shop, 514-842-2925, ext. 226, or www.therewaslight.ca.*

solemn occasions Montrealers put aside their differences and come together at the Basilica of Notre Dame. Having lost their secular power under the British, the Sulpicians sought to reinforce their religious prominence with a grand cathedral, where the faithful of Montreal could gather.

They commissioned an Irish American, James O'Donnell, who designed twin-towered Notre Dame in Gothic Revival style. Construction began in 1824 and the Basilica opened in 1829, but it wasn't yet finished—work continued until 1870. The cathedral marked the first large-scale use of limestone in Montreal, which became a signature building material in the city.

The Cathedral – Outside, the church is an expression of grandeur and a projection of power; inside, it is opulent and spiritual at the same

Notre Dame Basilica

©Richard Nowitz/Apa Publications

Place des Arts on summer evening

©Yves Renaud/Place des Arts

time, and simply overpowering in the otherworldly play of natural light flowing in through its three rose windows. The woodwork is sumptuous, painted and gilt, cascading into niches filled with saints. Decorations are largely of carved pine and oak. The lower stained-glass windows, crafted in Limoges, France, tell the story of Montreal. The **organ** is one of the largest anywhere. At the rear of the cathedral, the modern **Sacred Heart Chapel** contrasts sharply with the rest of Notre Dame. The chapel was reconstructed in contemporary style, with light wood paneling, following a fire in 1978. Not to be missed.

PLACE DES ARTS★★

260, Rue de Maisonneuve West.
www.laplacedesarts.com.
Open year-round daily and for
performances. Métro Place des
Arts, green line.

In the 1960s, the city of Montreal selected what used to be a no-man's land for its performance center, between the English business section in the west and the traditional French cultural

institutions along Rue Saint-Denis. The first of the government-sponsored mega-projects of Montreal, it was followed by nearby Complexe Guy-Favreau and the monumental concrete **Olympic Stadium**, built for the 1976 Olympic Games.
Events flow around the fountains and through the multilevel

What's Doing at the *Place*?

Any time the weather's mild, there's sure to be a festival at Place des Arts. Stages are set up in the surrounding streets during the Jazz Festival and the open areas filled with souvenir shops, refreshment stands, stages, inflatables, and people, people, people. During the annual Film Festival, spectators unfold chairs and set down blankets to get comfy and watch an outdoor movie. As the entire PDA area has been reinvented into **Quartier des Spectacles** (Entertainment District), it now includes **Place des Festivals** on Rue Jeanne-Mance, **Promenade des Artists** along Rue de Maisonneuve, and **Le Partérre** on Rue St. Urbain.

LANDMARKS

plazas of Place des Arts during the milder months and even in the middle of winter. Glass walls allow a view inside to Salle Wilfrid Pelletier and the **Contemporary Art Museum★★** *(Musée d'Art Contemporain de Montréal; see Museums).*

Salle Wilfrid Pelletier – At the north end of the plaza is the home of Opéra de Montréal and Les Grands Ballets. A large columned building with a curving facade, it is also the venue of choice for Broadway road shows and international music acts.

The **Montreal Symphony Hall** is the new structure east of PDA plaza and home to the Orchestre Symphonique (Montreal Symphony Orchestra).

Théâtre Maisonneuve – Located near Rue Sainte-Catherine, this large performance facility lies directly above the **Théâtre Jean-Duceppe**. The floating floor of one is also the moveable ceiling of the space below—but the construction

is such that nobody is aware of the activity in the other hall. To reach any of these, or the smaller **Studio Théâtre** or **Cinquième Salle**, enter the indoor passageway that descends from Rue Sainte-Catherine *(see Performing Arts).*

MARY QUEEN OF THE WORLD CATHEDRAL★★
Cathédrale Marie-Reine-du-Monde

Corner Rue Mansfield & Boul. René-Lévesque. 514 866-1661. www.cathedralecatholiquede montreal.org. Mon–Fri 7am–6pm, Sat 7.30am–6pm, Sun 8.30am–6pm. Summer tours. Métro Bonaventure.

Rarely does a city have more than one Catholic cathedral, but the establishment of a large Catholic church in the very center of 19C Montreal's English-dominated business district was a political and cultural statement by the bishop of the day, Ignace Bourget. And what a statement! Plans were unblushingly copied from those of St. Peter's in Rome, reduced to half-scale. Work began in 1870, but with money coming in and running out, it was not until 1894 that the cathedral formally opened.

The Building – Even on a reduced scale, "St.-Peter's-in-Montreal" is massive, successfully competing for attention with some of Montreal's tallest buildings nearby. Copper-plated statues in the pediment represent the patron saints of local parishes. Inside, the gold-plated copper canopy is a replica of one in St. Peter's in Rome. Check out the woodwork and the series of paintings that reveal French-Canadian history.

Mary Queen of the World Cathedral
©Richard Nowitz/Apa Publications

PLACE MONTRÉAL TRUST★★

1500 Ave. McGill College at Rue Ste-Catherine. 514-843-8000. Open year-round Mon–Tue 10am–6pm (Jun–Aug until 8pm), Wed–Fri 10am–9pm, Sat 10am–5pm, Sun 11am–5pm. Métro McGill, green line, and Peel via Underground City.

Place Montréal Trust

Lili Thérault/MICHELIN

Dating from 1989, the Montreal Trust tower is a remarkable intersection of cylindrical volumes, and of materials old and new. Flat surfaces are mostly of rose-colored marble, divided by cylinders of glass and polished aluminum—the one indistinguishable from the other—reflecting the sky, clouds and surrounding cityscape. The effect, on a sunny day, is a remarkable illusion of translucence and depth. Inside, Place Montréal Trust is dedicated to materialism. It extends well below street level and connects with the Underground City. The purpose is shopping—there are scores of boutiques—but the architectural drama of five stories of galleries, the play of water from one of the largest indoor fountains anywhere, the street scene visible in any weather through expanses of plate glass, and refreshment at numerous eateries may entice you to stay longer.

PLACE VILLE-MARIE★★

Ave. McGill College at Rue Cathcart. 514-861-9393. Métro McGill, green line, or Bonaventure, orange line (www.placevillemarie.com).

Place Ville-Marie *(PVM in local usage)* marked a Canadian advance in urban design when it opened in 1962. Predecessors such as the Dominion Square Building included interior shopping along arcades.

Eaton Centre
Ave. McGill College at Rue Ste-Catherine.
Just across Avenue McGill College and a few steps past the corner **(going eastward, north side)** is the earlier **Eaton Centre**, another multistory, contemporary shopping complex. It adjoins the stately Art-Deco building of the legendary **Eaton Department Store**, which fell victim to downmarket competition and closed its doors a few years ago. The space has been taken over by other retailers and traces of the original interior styling remain.

©Eaton Centre

LANDMARKS

But Place Ville-Marie reached out underground to connect with adjacent urban nodes, such as Central Station. On the surface, it blurred boundaries, encouraging pedestrians to flow onto its plazas, and onward to its shopping arcades through multiple wide doorways. Aluminum sheathing marked a departure from stone, brick, and steel surfacing materials.

Long delayed by lack of funds, Place Ville-Marie was one of the greatest construction projects in Canada of its day, filling a gaping basin left in the center of downtown by railway tunnel construction.

Beacon of Montreal – Place Ville-Marie now soars over Montreal in counterpoint to the great mass of Mount Royal. The cruciform plan of the Royal Bank Tower reflects the cross of faith that crowns the mountain. At night, the cross shines on Mount Royal, as does the beacon atop Place Ville-Marie .

The Buildings and the Plan – The Royal Bank Tower★ *(Tour Banque-Royale)*, at 42 stories, is the largest of PVM's buildings, designed by the firm of I. M. Pei.

Smaller buildings partially flank the complex. Generous street-level interruptions allow the unimpeded flow of pedestrians.

Visiting – Just walk in! Enter Place VilleMarie from the freestanding glassed-in entry on the plaza, through doors on Rue Cathcart or Rue University, or by passageway from Central Station or the Eaton Centre. Shops, restaurants, and occasional entertainment are sufficient to keep you occupied for hours; light flowing in through the skylights makes the ambience downright cheery.

ST. JOSEPH'S ORATORY★★
Oratoire Saint-Joseph

3800 Chemin Queen-Mary. 514-733-8211. www.saint-joseph.org. Votive Chapel open year-round daily 6am–9.30pm; Basilica open May–Nov daily 7am–9pm & for late Masses; Way of the Cross Gardens open May–Oct. Métro Côte-des-Neige, blue line, and 166 bus.

No other religious site in Montreal comes close to St. Joseph's in massive size or in the devotion

Place VilleMarie

© Tibor Bognar/Age Fotostock

St. Joseph's Oratory

Pierre Etheir/MICHELIN

of its visitors. Saint Brother André (1845–1937), who began his religious life as a porter in a school, promoted the healing power of praying to St. Joseph. He attracted a following, who threw off their crutches and afflictions in ever greater numbers. Saint Brother André was canonized in 2010.

The Oratory – Construction of the Oratory—literally, a place of prayer—began in 1924 on the northern slope of Westmount Mountain. The massive project was interrupted a number of times, finally coming under the direction of renowned Benedictine architect Paul Bellot. It was not completed until 1967. You can reach the Romanesque Oratory on foot by a series of staircases ascending its terraced lawns (or you can drive). It rises to 154m/505ft above the city. The space under the dome soars to 60m/198ft, while the tip of its crowning cross stands 97m/320ft above the ground.

Inside, St. Joseph's is stark and powerful, barely adorned, and suited to private prayer and meditation. The carillon is from France, originally intended for installation in the Eiffel Tower

(performances Wed through Sun and workshops too). Not incidentally, with the Oratory''s new elevators and dome terrace, the commanding **views** northward over the city to the Laurentian Mountains are not to be missed.

The Votive Chapel – The most moving testimony to the powers of St. Joseph is the collection of canes and crutches left by those cured through prayer. Enlarged several times to accommodate his followers, Saint Brother André's original **chapel** has been restored to its appearance in 1904.

Way of the Cross – The traditional pilgrims' route along the hillside is marked by 42 statues designed by Louis Parent, one of Quebec's most noted contemporary sculptors. The statue of St. John at Gethsemane is considered an Art-Deco masterpiece.

SUN LIFE BUILDING★★

1155 Rue Metcalfe. Métro Peel, green line, or Bonaventure, orange. www.edificesunlife.ca.

Towering over the east side of Dorchester Square, the massive and bankerly Sun Life Building was the

LANDMARKS

largest of the British Empire when it was completed in 1933. Designed by the firm of Darling and Pearson, the monumental edifice sports columns and pediments that make reference to classical architecture but they are out of proportion—the effect is something like a cubist painting. It's only a step from the Sun Life Building to architectural designs that recognize the skyscraper as a class unto itself.

Bastion for Britain – Headquarters of a major insurance company, "la Sun Life du Canada," secure in fact as well as symbolically, the Sun Life Building came to hold the gold reserves of several European countries during World War II. With the outbreak of the war, the building's lower basement was modified to house the securities of the British Government. Sent overseas at great risk in 1940 and placed under constant guard, much of Britain's wealth was secretly kept here.

Sun Life Building
©Gregory B. Gallagher/Michelin

BANK OF MONTREAL★
Banque de Montréal

119 Rue St-Jacques Ouest. 514-877-6810. Métro Place-d'Armes, orange line (www.bmo.com).

There have always been moneylenders, but the Bank of Montreal was the first proper bank in Canada as of 1819.

By 1847, it was dominant enough to establish a new head office on Place d'Armes, the most prestigious location of the day. British architect John Wells designed a domed secular temple that imitated the Pantheon in Rome. John Steele later added the sculptures on the pediment. The premises were enlarged in 1901 while preserving the dome as the centerpiece. A vast, columned hall still provides retail services.

To the left of the entry, a one-room free **museum** displays antique adding machines and photos of banking operations in times past *(open year-round Mon–Fri 10am–4pm)*.

Building as Logo – Early on, the bank realized the value of architecture as symbol and brand. Branches began to appear in major centers across Canada, differing in detail but always faithful to the dome and columns as symbols of strength, security, and reliability.

🐟 BIODÔME★

4777 Ave. Pierre-de-Coubertin. 514-868-3000. www.biodome. qc.ca. Open year-round Tue–Sun 9am–5pm (summer daily until 6pm). $16.50 or $28.00 for Nature Package (Biodome, Insectarium, & Botanical Gardens). Métro Viau, green line.

Biodôme
Pierre Etheir/MICHELIN

vines and ferns, swim, fly, grow, and climb through the tropics, the Laurentian forest, the St. Lawrence River, and the refrigerated Arctic. A **free shuttle** provides transportation between the Biodôme, the Insectarium, Botanical Garden, Olympic Park, and Viau Métro station.

CITY HALL★
Hôtel de Ville

275 Rue Notre-Dame Est. 514-872-0077. Open for self-guided tours Mon–Fri 8am–5pm; or guided tours Mon–Fri 9am–4pm by appointment. 514-872-0077. Closed holidays. Métro Champ-de-Mars, orange line. www.vieux.montreal.qc.ca

Montreal's City Hall is a solid, stone-clad building with a mansard roof, the first major building in the city to adopt the Second Empire style that was all the rage toward the end of the 19C. Completed in 1878,

Pack up the world's climates and place them under a dome—a former Olympic cycling track—for all the world to see. It sounds like the project of a mad scientist, but it's fairly amazing in reality. At the Biodôme, caimans and piranhas, penguins and parrots,

Remnants of New France

Now used for lunchtime breaks by office workers, the open space to the north of **City Hall** is a one-time military drill area called the Champs de Mars. The newly exposed parallel stone wall trench reveals the original security system that once surrounded the settlement. To the north you can see the gentle rise of land that forms part of the Montreal Escarpment, the ridge that runs the length of the island. Beyond is the skyline of downtown Montreal, the newer part of the city along Rue Sainte-Catherine that flourished in the latter part of the 19C.

Pierre Etheir/MICHELIN
City Hall

LANDMARKS

51

it was raised one story in 1922 during reconstruction after a fire. Controversies surrounding City Hall are usually of local concern only, but in 1967, President Charles de Gaulle of France called out *"Vive le Québec libre"* ("Long live free Quebec") from the balcony, giving new life to the secessionist movement and setting off a chill in Canada–France relations that lasted for years.

Decorative Flourishes – Noted art works in City Hall include the bronze *The Sower and Woman with Bucket* by Alfred Laliberté. A large bronze chandelier illuminates the main hall *(hall d'honneur)*. In the Council Chamber, stained-glass windows illustrate street scenes of Montreal in the 1920s.

COMPLEXE DES JARDINS★

150 Rue Ste-Catherine Ouest. 514-845-4636. www.complexedes jardins.com. Open year-round Mon–Wed 9.30am–6pm, Thu–Fri 9.30am–9pm, Sat 9.30am–5pm, Sun noon–5pm (Métro level Food Court open every day, 6 or 7am– 8 or 9pm). Métro Place des Arts, green line.

When Complexe Desjardins opened in 1976, combining government offices and private enterprises, it immediately broke the mold. Gone are the long passageways of earlier underground centers. Complexe Desjardins revolves around a vast multistory interior cavern, diving down several levels below the street and soaring to cathedral heights. It's an indoor continuation of the terraces of Place des Arts across the way, and

Complexe Desjardins

©André Rider

the activity—from shopping to rushing to a concert or multimedia presentation—is virtually non-stop. Enter through the doors on Rue Sainte-Catherine, or underground from the Métro, or if you're staying in the Hyatt Regency Hotel, take the glass-sided elevator from upstairs into the cavern, or from the carport entrance on Rue Jeanne-Mance.

Counter-Complexe – Across Boulevard René Lévesque to the south is the federal government's counterpoint to the provincially owned Complexe Desjardins. **Complexe Guy-Favreau** is red brick on the outside, all utilitarian passageways on the inside, and an assortment of federal offices upstairs in the six connected blocks. Together, Complexe Guy-Favreau, Place des Arts, and Complexe Desjardins form an eastern suburb of Montreal's **Underground City** *(see pp 56–57).*

DOMINION SQUARE BUILDING★

1010 Rue Ste-Catherine.
Métro Peel, green line.

The Dominion Square Building was an innovator at the time of its inauguration on the eve of the stockmarket crash of 1929. It follows Renaissance Revival stylistic dictates, with clearly defined top, middle, and base sections. But for its height, the structure would blend into a Florentine streetscape. In its details, however, this building was at the avant-garde of adapting to the extremes of the climate. Its insets brought natural light to offices inside, even on dreary days. The shopping arcade, protected from the extremes of weather, was a precursor to urban indoor malls. Tourisme Québec's **Infotouriste Centre** counter is located here with info for visitors: *514-873-2015 (www.bonjourquebec.com).*

DORCHESTER SQUARE★

Bounded by Rue Metcalfe, Rue Peel & Boul. René-Lévesque. Métro Peel, green line; or Bonaventure, orange line.

Dorchester Square is a green, leafy, and pleasant expanse. With adjoining Place du Canada to the south, it forms the largest open area of Central Montreal. The one-time cemetery for cholera victims lies at the center of what was once considered the dominant "Anglo" business area of Montreal, Quebec, and Canada.

The park itself—called Dominion Square until a few years ago—tells Canadian history from a federalist viewpoint, which in Quebec is not the whole story.

The major thoroughfare bordering the south of the square was once named Dorchester Boulevard for Sir Guy Carleton, Lord Dorchester, the governor who secured the allegiance of French Canadians by protecting their land rights, religion, and civil laws.

The road now bears the name of René Lévesque, who as provincial leader sought to take Quebec out of Canada.

©Gregory B. Gallagher/Michelin

Dorchester Square

LANDMARKS

To the north, east and south stand some of the most impressive structures of the first half of the 20C in Canada.

HABITAT '67★

2600 Ave. Pierre-Dupuis, Cité-du-Havre. www.habitat67.com.

Completed in time for the World Exposition of 1967, this remarkable "concept" apartment complex (in the manner of concept cars) was designed by young architect Moshe Safdie and constructed on the embankment that protects Montreal's port. Safdie took a page from the methods of automakers and had the apartment units fabricated on an assembly line. They were set in place at odd angles to form an open complex. Habitat 67 is best viewed from Old Montreal, or the street in front of it that leads to St. Helen's Island and Casino Montreal.

One-Off – Unfortunately, Habitat '67 proved unsuitable for the era of high energy prices that followed soon after its completion, but it did inspire others to go against the grain. It's not unusual to spot an apartment building in Montreal that's more pyramidal than rectangular. And right next to Habitat is **Tropiques Nord**, a more recent building with a greenhouse extending over the entire riverside exposure. More development is approved for this dreamy waterside area.

McGILL UNIVERSITY★

805 Rue Sherbrooke Ouest. 514-398-6555. www.mcgill.ca. Métro McGill, green line.

An oasis of lawns, trees, and temples of learning, venerable McGill University occupies an enviable downtown campus, where Montreal slopes upward onto Mount Royal. The oldest university in Canada—consistently top-rated—was chartered by King George IV in 1821, with start-up funds provided by the estate of Glasgow-born fur trader James McGill. The university now occupies 80 buildings spread across downtown and the MacDonald campus of agricultural studies at the western end of the island. More than 34,000 students are enrolled.

Habitat '67

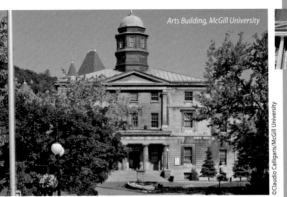

Arts Building, McGill University

©Claudio Calligaris/McGill University

🚶 **Campus Walk** – Start your stroll through the campus at the Roddick Gates on Rue Sherbrooke West, erected in 1924.

Walk up the central drive to appreciate the main buildings, named for illustrious teachers, alumni, and benefactors ranging from Peter Redpath to William Shatner of *Star Trek* fame.

The **Redpath Museum of Natural History**★ *(see Museums)* stands to the west of the drive.

At the far end, the **Arts Building** is the oldest on campus, the work of noted architect John Ostell.

RITZ-CARLTON HOTEL★

1228 Rue Sherbrooke Ouest. 514-842-4212. www.ritzmontreal.com. Métro Peel, green line.

Grande Dame of the Golden Square Mile, this was the first built by César Ritz in North America. A true Renaissance Revival opened in 1912, it remains unchallenged as the epitome of elegance in the north, especially with the newest renovations adding a residential element. Take a quick look inside at the lobby paneled in dark wood,

with leather banquettes and brass detailing. Or stay for lunch in the **Café de Paris**, or take high English tea in the **Jardin du Ritz** (Ritz Garden) with its signature duck pond.

ROYAL BANK OF CANADA★
Banque Royale du Canada

360 Rue St-Jacques Ouest. Open Mon–Fri 10am–4pm. Métro Square-Victoria, orange line. www.rbc.com.

Montreal's skyline soared after 1924, when a height limit was repealed. Formerly Merchant's Bank of Halifax, new Royal Bank of Canada HQ was completed by 1926, with New York-style setbacks and traditional Renaissance tiers stretched to its full 20 stories *(the first to be built higher than Notre-Dame Basilica)*.

The base was modeled after the Teatro San Carlo in Naples. Pass through the polished brass doors under an ornate arched entry, into the lobby with its great arches, chandeliers, coffered ceiling, and lively blue, pink, and gilt décor.

LANDMARKS

55

⚜ UNDERGROUND CITY (Ville Souterraine)
(www.voyagefute.ca)

Running beneath streets, threading between buildings, surfacing in multistoried plazas diving way down to Métro level is Montreal's Underground City, or RÉSO. Seven major hotels, 200 restaurants, museums, rail stations, bus terminals, cinemas, nightclubs, and even a library lie along the pedestrian network.

There are busy thoroughfares and quiet corners, hubs of transportation, and palaces of commerce. Over 500,000 people pass through each day. As in the city above, the Underground Pedestrian Network has its neighborhoods, ranging from upscale to workaday. Renovation is ongoing, along with controversy over designs. Trends at the beginning favored keeping out the world above. More recently, light wells have pierced the netherworld. The Underground City began with passageways in and under Place VilleMarie , completed in 1962. Tunnels snaked southward to join with Central Station. A cheery, village-like web of shops unfolds, including sidewalk cafes.

As new exhibition centers and shopping areas opened, the Underground City extended its arms to welcome them: westward to Place Bonaventure and Windsor Station; northward to Les Cours

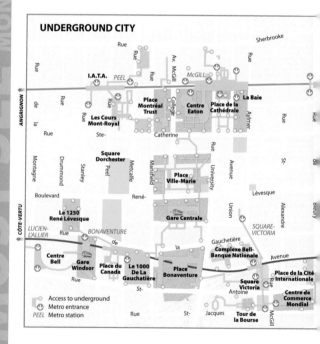

Mont-Royal, Place Montréal Trust, the Eaton Centre, and Promenades de la Cathédrale; and most recently, east beyond the Stock Exchange Tower and the Montreal World Trade Centre to the Palais des Congrès.

On a snowy day, you can enter the Underground City on the edge of Old Montreal and surface all the way up north at Rue Sherbrooke. And you can access your hotel, eat in fine restaurants, enjoy a movie or show, and end the day without having once stepped outside.

As with above-ground towns, the success of the main axis has spurred rival developments. A second underground axis runs southward from Place des Arts to Complexe Desjardins, Complexe Guy-Favreau, and the Palais des Congrès *(Convention Center)* south of Chinatown, then loops west to the original underworld. And a smaller, but sophisticated rival consists largely of the passages running under and through the Université de Québec à Montréal campus around Rue Saint-Denis and Rue Sainte-Catherine.

If past is prologue, these too will one day interconnect with the main network.

Be sure to take along a map during your wanderings—the twists and turns can rival those of a medieval city, leaving you closer to your starting point than you meant to be.

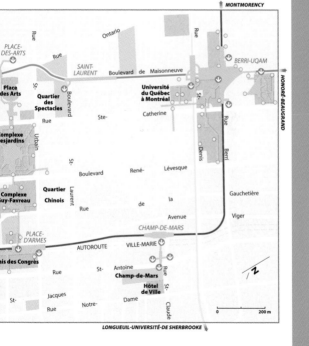

57

MUSEUMS

A number of Montreal's museums are world-class, and some, such as the Canadian Centre for Architecture, have no peer anywhere. Others are off-beat or just plain fun. Perhaps best of all, the museum experience in Montreal is on a human scale. You can see a fair part of most collections in a few hours and linger at items that interest you without feeling rushed to see it all.

CONTEMPORARY ART MUSEUM★★
Musée d'Art Contemporain de Montréal

185 Rue Ste-Catherine Ouest. 514-847-6226. www.macm.org. Open year-round Tue–Sun and holiday Mondays, 11am–6pm (Wed 11am–9pm). $10 (free Wed 5–9pm). Métro Place-des-Arts, green line.

There's only one cultural complex in Canada devoted to both the performing and visual arts – Place des Arts – and this museum is a major part of the PDA family. Everything in the building dates from 1939 and after.

The emphasis is on Canadian art, especially big-name Quebeckers. The likes of Jean-Paul Riopelle and Paul-Émile Borduas—some of whose works fall between Picasso and Native American symbolism—

Such a Deal

The **Montreal Museums Pass** provides entry to 38 city museums on three consecutive days for $60 *($65 with transit pass)*, including taxes.

That amounts to the admission price at three major museums alone. The pass is available at most museum ticket counters and tourist information centers. Many museums also offer family rates for two adults and two children, as well as discounts for seniors, students, and children. *www.montrealmuseums.org.*

may at times be seen in Paris and London, but never in such concentration as in the Musée d'Art Contemporain.

But this is no palace of dead painters: the permanent collection

Contemporary Art Museum

McCord Museum

©McCord Museum/Tourisme Montréal

includes sculpture, photographs, prints, and installations. The museum lives modern art by staging multimedia events, new dance, experimental theater, contemporary music, video, and film . . . and all this as a former department of the provincial government—proof that Quebec is, indeed, different.

Now very much at the hub of the newly expanded Quartier des spectacle concept, the formerly stark west side of the MAC now brims with life in new bistros, and front and center on the new festival pedestrian concourse. Waterfalls, live concerts, and light shows only add to the museum's relevance. Don't forget to have a delicious lunch or dinner at **Restaurant Le C** onsite. Enter the museum from the east side or via the sheltered concourse of Place des Arts *(see Performing Arts).*

McCORD MUSEUM★★
Musée McCord

690 Rue Sherbrooke Ouest. 514-398-7100. www.mccord-museum. qc.ca. Open year-round Tue–Fri 10am–6pm; weekends 10am–5pm; also holiday Mondays & July–Sept Mon 10am–5pm. $13. Métro McGill, green line, or bus 24.

The Collections – How did people dress 150 years ago during Montreal's winter? How did Native Canadians cook and sew and build?

Strolling Avenue McGill College

One of the shortest streets in Montreal, **Avenue McGill College** became one of the widest only a few years back simply to provide a dramatic approach to McGill University and a broad vista of Mount Royal. Such are priorities in Montreal, where appearances and **grandeur** count.

Kiosks, display cases, and public art adorn the broad sidewalks of the avenue, turning it into Montreal's greatest open-air museum. The most attention-grabbing piece is **The Illuminated Crowd**, a throng of comic-style humans molded in polymers by Raymond Mason, in front of no. 1981 Avenue McGill College. When not functioning as a thoroughfare, the avenue closes off easily at either end to become a plaza or handy setting for political demonstrations.

MUSEUMS

You'll find the answers here in this wonderful collection of Quebec artifacts.

The McCord has everything from records of the fur trade to cartoons from modern Montreal newspapers, and the museum's new brand, **McCord Museum, Our People, Our Stories**, selects from this treasure trove to present a portrait of how Montrealers lived over the years. Daily life unfolds through dresses and formal outfits, hunting equipment, everyday objects from glassware to hoop skirts, and a sampling from a fabulous stock of period toys.

The Notman Archives – View ordinary, infamous and extraordinary Montrealers, from over 100 years ago. Photographer William Notman immortalized them all on film over a period of 78 years until his death in 1891.

Current Traveling Exhibitions – Materials selected from the museum's collection bring past and remote lives into the present for museums across Canada. The legendary *After Notman; Photographic Views of Montreal,*

together with *Haida Art,* and *Clothes Make the MAN* entertain while touring. Look out for an exhibition from the McCord coming to a museum near you.

POINTE-À-CALLIÈRE; MONTREAL MUSEUM OF ARCHAEOLOGY AND HISTORY★★
Musée d'Archéologie et d'Histoire de Montréal— Pointe-à-Callière

350 Place Royale at Rue de la Commune. 514-872-9150. http://pacmuseum.qc.ca. Open late-Jun–Sep Mon–Fri 10am–6pm, weekends 11am–6pm. Rest of the year Tue–Fri 10am–5pm, weekends 11am–5pm. $15. Métro Place d'Armes, orange line.

If you think of history as dusty books and even dustier costumes, think again. The Pointe-à-Callière Museum manages to be futuristic and fascinating while literally diving into the past. It's not only about history, it *is* history— located right where Samuel de

Pointe-à-Callière - Musée d'archéologie et d'histoire de Montréal

©Normand Rajotte, Pointe-à-Callière

Musée des Beaux-Arts de Montréal, Pavillon Jean-Noel Desmarais

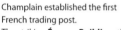

Champlain established the first French trading post.

The striking **Éperon Building**, the visible tip of the museum, faces the harbour; its railings, terraces, and smooth surfaces are like the decks, hull, and superstructure of a ship. A multimedia presentation—complete with actors, props, lights and sound effects—traces the history of Montreal, beginning with the Ice Age. The third-floor terrace and **Restaurant l'Arrivage** provide some of the best **views** of the port. **Archaeological Crypt** – Head down from the main building to delve into history. Directly below Place Royale are the excavations of the original French trading post. It's all now stabilized, climate-controlled, illuminated, and partially reconstructed. Visitors walk along the former bed of the Little St. Pierre River (later vaulted as the town sewer), through the first public square and to the partially excavated remains of Montreal's first Christian cemetery. Sound and video are projected right onto the ruins to bring the old marketplace to life. **Old Customs House** *(l'Ancienne Douane)* – The passageway through the crypt leads to the Old Customs House, completed in Neoclassical style in 1838 according to a design by John Ostell. The Customs House, emblematic of Montreal's importance as a British port, houses an exhibit on world trade, as well as the museum gift shop.

The **Youville Pumping Station** *(173 Place d'Youville)* is the city's first electrical pumphouse and presents Scottish and English ingenuity in the early 20C.

MONTREAL MUSEUM OF FINE ARTS★★

Musée des Beaux-Arts de Montréal

1380 Rue Sherbrooke Ouest at Rue Crescent. 514-285-2000. www.mmfa.qc.ca. Open year-round Tue 11am–5pm, Wed–Fri 11am–9pm, weekends 10am–5pm. Closed Jan 1 & Dec 25. $15 (half-price Wed evening). Métro Guy-Concordia, green line, or bus 24.

The Fine Arts Museum is to Montreal what the Metropolitan is to New York—dignified,

The Other Side of the Street: The Desmarais Building

On the south side of **Rue Sherbrooke**, the facade of the newer, contemporary section of the museum is a monumental sculpture in itself, the glass eye of a window set into a largely blank wall. Architect Moshe Safdie showed little respect for convention, blurring the borders between indoors and out with a soaring greenhouse foyer, but even masters make mistakes. The stairways, with ultra-short risers, are disorienting – keep to the elevators. Temporary exhibitions, along with works from the permanent collection, fill the huge, flexible spaces.

comprehensive, authoritative—but far more human in scale and presentation. A few hours here will give you an appreciation of the art of Canada and Quebec.

Hornstein Building – The original museum is a 1912 Beaux Arts monument faced in white marble. Beyond the colonnade and portico are a grand staircase and newer galleries in the Stewart Pavilion.

Canadian Collection – The long-awaited Claire and Marc Bougie Pavilion houses an expanded Canadian Collection, including many new Quebec masterpieces. You'll see Inuit art, paintings by the Group of Seven, and works by Montrealers James Wilson Morrice, Ozias Leduc, and Alfred Laliberté, among others. The museum purchased the former Erskine and American Church (1894) and have created a singular new concert hall featuring the church's famed 118 **Tiffany** stained-glass windows. A **Sculpture Garden** tops the new development. Free admission for all to this new pavilion.

Decorative Arts – A top drawing card is the collection of European and Canadian decorative arts. Holdings represent every major trend, from Art Nouveau to post-Modernism.

Underground Museum – As a true Montreal institution the museum plunges into passageways and halls that connect its two main buildings, right under Rue Sherbrooke. The **Galleries of Ancient Cultures** showcase masks and ritual objects from Africa and Oceania, porcelain from China, Indian sculpture, and pre-Columbian ceramics.

BIOSPHÈRE CANADA★

160 Chemin Tour-de-l'Isle, Île Ste-Hélène. 514-283-5000. www.ec.gc.ca/biosphere. Open Jun–Nov daily 10am–6pm. Rest of year Tue–Fri 10am–5pm; weekends, holidays, and school breaks 10am–5pm. Closed Jan 1 & Dec 25–26. $12. Métro Parc Jean-Drapeau, yellow line, or Jacques-Cartier Bridge. Tours available daily.

Once the United States pavilion at Expo '67, this wonder of modern architecture was reborn in 1995 as the Biosphère. Since then, it reigns as the only museum on the continent devoted to the environment in general, and the Great Lakes and St. Lawrence River in particular. Inside the geodesic dome, the levels of the museum rise like decks of a ship; an expanse of water lies directly below, and the St. Lawrence flows by on two sides—you're surrounded by the subject matter. In **Water Wonders!**

Biosphère Canada

© Tourisme Montréal

dive into the topic as you walk on water using floating skates, construct watercourses, generate energy, follow the daily quest for survival, and design, steer, and even sink a ship *(bring change of clothes)*.

Planète Bucky – Sustainable development focuses on inventions of dome creator Buckminster Fuller, including the streamlined Dymaxion car, the Dymaxion house, and even the super-efficient Dymaxion bathroom, as well as the Biosphère's own wastewater-treatment marsh. Try the cool **GeoTour 67** using **GPS** technology to tour the island *($5)*.

CANADIAN CENTRE FOR ARCHITECTURE★
Centre Canadien d'Architecture

1920 Rue Baile. 514-939-7026. www.cca.qc.ca. Open year-round Wed–Sun 11am–6pm (Thu until 9pm). $10 (free after 5.30pm Thu), including tour. Closed Jan 1 & Dec 25. Métro Guy-Concordia, green line.

Philanthropist, heiress, preservationist, and architect, Phyllis Lambert practices what she preaches! When the derelict Shaughnessy House was about to be flattened, she stepped in with her checkbook and professional skills, and saw to its loving and painstaking restoration. The mansion was to become the

Specifics
About the Sphere

♦ The geodesic dome is almost, but not quite a sphere. In fact, it is two structures: the outer layer is made up of triangles, the inner of smaller hexagons.

♦ The dome rises to 62.8m/206ft and encloses 189,724 cu m/1,700,000cu ft.

♦ Its frame is made of steel tubes welded to steel joints.

♦ The original dome was covered in (flammable!) acrylic panels.

♦ Constantly in touch with water, the newer museum is inspired by the river and laid out like a ship, complete with a hold, a bridge, and a crow's nest.

MUSEUMS

63

More Recycled Architecture

After the CCA, visit other Montreal architectural wonders nearby. **Le Faubourg Sainte-Catherine** *(1616 Rue Ste-Catherine Ouest; www.lefaubourg.com)* is a meeting of outlets of ready-to-eat exotic foods from the world over, along with specialty grocers and bakers in an open-plan, multilevel indoor neighborhood. Peek through the south windows to the heritage stone buildings of the **Grey Nuns Motherhouse**, now part of adjacent Concordia University, where travelers may rent accommodation during the summer months. *(http://vpservices.concordia.ca/summerhousing)*

centerpiece of a museum that celebrates public involvement in buildings and their design. Current exhibitions often focus on architecture from a specific era. CCA is also a research center with an unparalleled collection of prints, drawings, and photographs.

The Galleries – The new construction of CCA faces quiet Rue Baile with an imposing facade of granite and limestone. Despite the addition's mass, the galleries are relatively small-scale and interconnect in unpredictable ways.

Shaughnessy House – On the south side of the complex, this 1874 grande dame has been restored, adapted, and updated, with new floors and recessed lighting that's effective, if not historically accurate. The mansion houses the conservatory—delightful on a sunny winter's day—and the tearoom with Wi-Fi.

Sculpture Garden – Across busy Boulevard René-Lévesque, a plot of land isolated by expressway ramps is set with sculptures that suggest structures and elements of architecture, from an arcade that mirrors the Shaughnessy House to a homey, oversized chair of a long-gone dwelling, literally elevated to prominence.

MONTREAL HISTORY CENTRE★
Centre d'Histoire de Montréal

335 Place d'Youville. 514-872-3207. www2.ville.montreal.qc.ca/chm.htm. Open Tue–Sun 10am–5pm. Closed beginning of Jan. $6.00. Métro Square-Victoria, orange line, or bus 61.

Even before you walk into the History Centre on Place d'Youville, you're in Montreal as it used to be. The Grey Nuns Hospital *(Hôpital général des Sœurs Grises)* on the

Montreal History Centre

Pierre Etheir/MICHELIN

south side of Place d'Youville traces its history to the 18C. Just down the street, the 1820 Bouthillier warehouses present an elegant cut-stone, face and rough fieldstone workaday buildings in the courtyard past the coach gate. The square itself housed the Parliament of Canada—until rioters torched it in 1849.

Central Fire Station – The museum was once a fire station, but what a station! It was state-of-the-art for its day, with a drying tower just for hoses. Decked out in the Flemish style with decorative gable ends, the station has been a landmark from birth.

Permanent Exhibitions
Montreal Five Times takes you through the history of the city from the first fur trading post to the glory days of Expo '67 and the Olympics in the 1960s and 1970s. Through images, special effects, and objects, figures famous, infamous, and ordinary tell their stories and recreate their times.
Montreal of a Thousand Faces is a personal visit with Montrealers from the present and recent past. Settle into a period living room, or eavesdrop in an old-style kitchen, then walk into a general store, an office where typewriters still clack, or the cloakroom of a factory. Videotaped testimonies recount lives and experiences.
Up on the Roof – You can even do what you're usually not supposed to do—climb up to the roof for a look around the neighborhood from a daring perspective *(it's quite safe here—in an enclosed greenhouse-style gallery!)*.

MONTREAL'S OFFBEAT AND SPECIAL MUSEUMS

Every major city has an art museum or two, and probably some kind of science center, but how many have a museum entirely devoted to insects? A radio heritage museum, or a commemoration of the daily struggle in a poor neighborhood? No matter where your interests lie, at least one of these is sure to be a must-see for you.

La Musée du Château Dufresne★

2929 Rue Jeanne-d'Arc (Sherbrooke Street at Pie IX). 514-259-9201. www.chateaudufresne.com. Open year-round Wed–Sun 10am–5pm. $8. Métro Pie-IX, green line. Guided tours in the afternoon.

Once the home of the Decorative Arts Museum *(now absorbed by the Museum of Fine Arts)*, Château Dufresne has returned to its roots and exhibits itself for itself. It is the fine private *hôtel* (town mansion) of the merchant-prince Dufresne brothers, modeled after the Petit Trianon at Versailles. The Dufresnes were the patrons of "**Canada's Michaelangelo**": stained-glass master Guido Nincheri. There's nothing modest about this family home. Massive Ionic columns mark the facade; high windows and balconies suit a milder climate.
The bachelors Dufresne lived in separate wings decorated to their individual tastes—Marius, an architect and builder, favored oak paneling, while Oscar, who owned a shoe factory, preferred mahogany

MUSEUMS

65

La Musée du Château Dufresne

©Michel Gingras, Musée du Château Dufresne

and Italian marble. Period furniture and domestic objects decorate the château; all have been restored and located in their rightful places.

The Fur Trade at Lachine National Historic Site★
Lieu Historique National du Canada du Commerce-de-la-Fourrure-à-Lachine

1255 Boul. St-Joseph, Lachine. 514-637-7433. www.parcscanada. gc.ca/fourrure. $3.90. Open Apr–Nov 25 daily 9.30am–12.30pm &

The Fur Trade at Lachine National Historic Site

©Parks Canada

1pm–5pm (weekends until 6pm); early Oct–Nov Wed–Sun 9.30am–12.30pm & 1pm–5pm. Closed Dec–Mar & Nov 11. Métro Angrignon, green line, then bus 195.

The tale of the fur trade, the business that made Montreal, is told in a venerable stone warehouse, where pelts once arrived by river from the far reaches of the continent. Furs, fashion, and speculation drove prices to dizzying heights and calamitous crashes, as you'll learn here. Combine a visit with a cycling trip westward from downtown along the **Lachine Canal** *(see For Fun).*

Le Musée de Bronze de Montréal, Galerie d'Art
Montreal Bronze Museum & Art Gallery

Located inside the Maison Pierre du Calvet at 401 Rue Bonsecours. 514-282-1725. www.gaetantrottier.ca. Free admission.

A fascinating one-man creation by local artist/sculptor Gaetan Trottier, this museum-cum-art-gallery offers unusual exhibitions of both Trottier's metal works and paintings, and noted Quebec artists. Longtime resident of Old Montreal, Trottier's art and presence here is his legacy.

Redpath Museum of Natural History★
Musée d'Histoire Naturelle Redpath

859 Rue Sherbrooke Ouest, on the campus of McGill University. 514-398-4086. www.mcgill.ca/redpath. Open Mon–Fri 9am–5pm, Sun 1pm–5pm. Closed holidays. Métro McGill, green line, or bus 24.

Fossils, minerals, and stuffed species from the far corners of the world, but especially Canada and Quebec fill the Redpath. The ethnology collection contains 17,000 pieces from ancient Egypt, Equatorial Africa, Oceania, the Mediterranean, and South America. You'll find dinosaurs and mummies here, too. It's all in a lovely hall at McGill University: an unusual rounded classical temple with incongruous clerestory windows, a grand staircase, hardwood floors, and wainscoting.
The benefactor behind the building was Peter Redpath, whose name appears on most packaged sugar in Canada.

Écomusée du Fier Monde

2050 Rue Amherst. 514-528-8444. www.ecomusee.qc.ca. Open year-round Wed 11am–8pm, Thu & Fri 9.30am–4pm, weekends 10.30am–5pm. $6. Métro Berri-UQAM.

Once it was an Art-Deco public bath—complete with arched portals, brass friezes, and porthole windows—as well as a social center, and the pride of a gritty neighborhood, where most lodgings had no baths or showers. The moving story of the workers' daily lives, celebrations, meeting places, and churches is told through photos, documents, and the surrounding buildings *(ask about Sunday walking tours in summer)*.

Redpath Museum of Natural History

MUSEUMS

The Écomusée sits squarely in the Gay Village of today's Montreal. Huddled, tiny brick houses have been modernized with indoor plumbing, decorated with colorful paint, and gentrified with lovingly tended postage-stamp gardens—all quite a change from the not-so-glory days commemorated in the museum and a wholly different *fier monde* (proud world). Sits directly across from the new **Marché Saint-Jacques**, filled with fresh artisan goodies to eat onsite or to go.

Émile Berliner Radio Museum

Musée des Ondes Émile Berliner

1050 Rue Lacasse. 514-932-9663. www.berliner.montreal.museum. Open year-round Fri–Sun 2pm–5pm. $3. Métro Place Saint-Henri, orange line.

You listen to music on CDs and DVDs today, but it all began with the original gramophone invented by Émile Berliner. Flat records (recorded on one side only) and the Berliner Gramophone were first produced at a Montreal plant in 1900 and promoted using the trademark dog, Nipper. The company prospered, expanding into the most modern factory of its day in this industrial complex, and was eventually absorbed by RCA. Antique gramophones are on display in a section of the onetime RCA Victor plant. Prize pieces include models fitted into fine cabinetry, Edison's wax cylinder machines, and an RCA Victor Superheterodyne from 1935. Attendants will crank up the equipment so that you can appreciate state-of-the-art audio from a hundred years ago. Period advertisements tout the advantage of flat records over wax cylinders—a precursor to modern-day media wars.

Montreal Holocaust Memorial Centre

5151 Chemin de la Côte-Sainte-Catherine (Cummings House). 514-345-2605. www.mhmc.ca. Sun–Fri 10am–4pm, Wed until 9pm, $8. Entire museum wheelchair-accessible.

Dedicated to sensitizing everyone to racism, prejudice, and destruction through multimedia presentations about Jewish families past, present, and future. Learn about the cultural diversity of communities in Europe, North America, and beyond through presentation of their customs, rituals, and language. Survivor testimonials are especially poignant and create a sense of human dimension and scale. Guided tour recommended.

Rio Tinto Alcan Montreal Planetarium

1000 Rue St-Jacques West. 514-872-4530. www.planetarium.montreal. qc.ca. Hours vary seasonally. $8. Métro Bonaventure, orange line, or bus 107 on Rue Peel.

NOTE: Construction of the new building should be complete by March 2012. The new premises are located at the Olympic Park, allowing the site to join the other **Montreal Nature Museums**.

Stars rule! Montreal's planetarium *(also known as the Dow Planetarium after the brewing family that brought it to life)* is expectedly hemispherical on the outside. Inside, it's all state-of-the-art, with futuristic controls and sound system.

Shows most days range from holiday and children's themes to **Star Secrets** and **The Exotic Universe**. English-language presentations alternate with French *(call or check website for schedules)*.

La TOHU, Circus Arts Centre

2345 Rue Jarry, east, corner Iberville; Métro Jarry + 193 bus; 514-376-8648. Ticket office open daily 9am–5pm. Hand-to-Hand Package includes dining. www.tohu.ca.

One of the world's largest circus arts creation, training, distribution, and production centers. Partly financed by **Cirque du Soleil** *(the global HQ is here)*, and the **National Circus School**, this zone's mandate is multi-tiered: Circus, Earth, and People. Initially constructed to promote Montreal as a world center for the circus arts, it has become a major neighborhood reinvention concept, successfully rehabilitating the Saint-Michel Environmental Complex (former 182ha/450-acre landfilled Miron quarry).

Circus arts productions are performed in the round, with the entire development being one of the most amazing green architecture examples. Many free shows are scheduled each month, as well as performance workshops, circus history exhibitions, environmental events, and conferences.

Musée des Hospitaliéres de l'Hôtel-Dieu de Montréal

201 Avenue des Pins West, 514-849-2919, Métro Sherbrooke, then bus #144, or Métro Saint-Laurent and bus #55 north and walk west. Open Tue–Fri 10am–5pm, Sat & Sun 1pm–5pm, closed Mon. $6. Group tours by reservation.

This museum chronicles the history of medicine in Montreal, plus the first hospital next door to this site *(still in operation)*, and the co-founder, nurse Jeanne Mance. A staggering inventory of artifacts, medical instruments, and religious documents trace the work of both hospital and nurse. Visit the adjacent gardens and chapel, as well as the hospital for a full understanding of the importance of this site in the history of the city.

Montreal Canadiens Hall of Fame

Located inside the Centre Bell hockey complex, 1909 Avenue des Canadiens-de-Montréal. Métro Lucien-L'Allier, and Bonaventure. 514-925-7777. Tue–Sat 10am–6pm, Sun 12pm–5pm (non-game days). $10.50.

Mecca for anyone with a passion for ice hockey, this veritable museum documents the history of the most winning sports franchise on the planet. Interactive installations capture the spirit of the city, its working-class populace, and the sport invented two blocks from this site. Rare artifacts, photography, and even a Q&A session with legendary superstar Jean Beliveau add to a roster of treats for hockey fans.

MUSEUMS

PARKS AND GARDENS

They range from grand forests in the city (Mount Royal Park), to minutely planned gardens (La Fontaine Park), to sedate surprises in busy neighborhoods (Carré St-Louis), to reserves where raccoons and foxes share the wilderness with cross-country skiers (Cap St-Jacques Nature Park; *see For Fun*). Whether you want to people-watch, take a break from the city, or indulge in solitary meditation, Montreal has just the park.

MONTREAL BOTANICAL GARDEN★★
Jardin Botanique de Montréal

Corner Pie IX Street and Sherbrooke Street Est. 514-872-1400. www.ville.montreal.qc.ca/jardin. Open mid-May–mid-Sept daily 9am–6pm; mid-Sept–Oct 9am–9pm; Nov–mid-May Tue–Sun 9am–5pm (open holiday Mondays). Closed Jan 1 and Dec 24–25. Free guided tours daily except some Mondays 10am & 1.30pm (no tours in Oct). $16.50 mid-May–Oct 31, $14 winter, including **Insectarium** *onsite. Métro Viau, green line, then free shuttle or bus 185.*

Ranked among the world's finest horticultural facilities, Montreal's Botanical Garden holds over 22,000 species of plants, in 30 themed outdoor gardens, and protected in 10 oversized greenhouses. And all this in a winter city!

In northern latitudes, keeping the flowers in bloom is important stuff. A recent director of the garden, Pierre Bourque, went on to become mayor of Montreal. His on-the-job diplomatic experience included negotiating the construction of the Chinese Garden, in concert with officials from the People's Republic of China.

Flowery brook and pond, Montreal Botanical Garden

©Montréal Botanical Garden/Gilles Murray

Mount Royal Park

©Gregory B. Gallagher/Michelin

Garden Highlights
*Start at the reception garden.
A mini-train tours the site from
May–Oct.*

- No visitor can miss the **Chinese Garden**★, the largest outside China. It's authentic, even in its moon gateway, imported boulders and pavilions re-assembled by workers from Shanghai.

- **Conservatories**★ – The *serres d'exposition* follow geographical themes, from the Chinese greenhouse and "landscapes in pots" to a Mexican ranch, rain forest, and tropical plantations.

- The stately **Japanese Garden** includes a bonsai collection and emphasizes serenity and harmony through the interplay of plants, pebbles, and water. Tea ceremonies are held in the pavilion.

- Local species and bonsai grow inside the **Tree House**, while the **First Nations Garden** emphasizes the relationship of the Inuit and Amerindians with their natural surroundings.

🍁 MOUNT ROYAL PARK★★
Parc du Mont-Royal

Voie Camillien-Houde & Chemin Remembrance, directly north of downtown. 514-843-8240. www.lemontroyal.qc.ca. Open year-round daily 6am–midnight. Walk up Rue Peel, or Métro Mont-Royal, orange line, & bus 11.

Mount Royal *is* Montreal, in name and in spirit. Urban life without its mass and greenery is unimaginable.
A great park covers the upper slopes and valleys of the mountain. Forests, a lake, playing fields, and jogging and bicycle trails are just steps from the center of the city. If all this sounds like New York's Central Park, it's not by accident— both were designed by master landscape architect Frederick Law Olmstead.
But Mount Royal also has maple forests and lofty lookouts. In winter, skiers swish along cross-country trails on the flanks of the mountain, and up to and around the Cross, in their public, but very private

PARKS AND GARDENS

71

wood. Except for a single road (*Voie Camillien-Houde/Chemin Remembrance*), Mount Royal Park is closed to vehicles.

Best of the Park

Beaver Lake (*Lac aux Castors*), near the park's western edge, is deep enough for pedal boats in summer, and freezes quickly in winter to become a favorite skating rink (*see Musts for Fun*). Equipment rentals inside the chalet, plus delicious snacks and even fine dining at **Le Pavilion**. The **ski lift** in the meadow beyond operates on weekends.

Smith House (*Maison Smith*), at the foot of an escarpment off the transverse road, is a venerable stone structure from 1858. Stop by to view the exhibit on the mountain's ecology, flora, and fauna, and to warm up over a hot beverage, fresh soups, and sweets. The **Chalet, aka Kondiaronk Belevedere** is a more substantial

stone building on the edge of the slope facing downtown, with a **lookout** (*belvédère*) and **views★★★** toward the Green Mountains of Vermont. Illuminated at night, the 37m/120ft-high **cross** (*follow the path from Smith House or the Chalet*) recalls a wooden cross erected in thanksgiving after Montreal was spared a flood in 1643.

Camillien Houde Lookout faces the flatlands of eastern Montreal toward the Olympic Stadium and Montreal Tower.

NOTRE DAME ISLAND★
Île Notre-Dame

Access via Pont de la Concorde (Concorde Bridge).

This former embankment along the St. Lawrence Seaway was expanded with fill from excavations for Montreal's Métro (subway), just in time for Expo '67, the 1967 World's Fair. A bridge joins it with St. Helen's Island (although there is often no vehicular access from one to the other).

The principal attraction is the **Montreal Casino** (*see For Fun*), the former French pavilion at Expo '67, which resembles a foreshortened ship. At the western end of the island, the **beach** encircles an artificial lake, filled with water from St. Lawrence River that is largely cleansed by the plants in an adjacent lagoon.

Flower Power – An international gardening competition, the **Floralies**, was once held on Notre Dame Island—and never closed. One of Montreal's most enchanting surprises, it displays exotic gardens with regional themes, planted along a series of canals.

Montreal Casino, Notre Dame Island

©Richard Nowitz/Apa Publications

ST. HELEN'S ISLAND★
Île Ste-Hélène

Access via Pont Jacques-Cartier (Jacques-Cartier Bridge). Keep to the right. Automobiles are directed to parking lots on Île Ste-Hélène; through traffic to the Concorde Bridge may be restricted.

This former military outpost sports a **marina** and **lake** at the eastern tip, site of a spectacular fireworks competition on summer weekends. Quebec's most modern outdoor pools, built for the 2005 World Aquatic Championships, invite swimmers, while a forest with a pond and falls offers seclusion. Most significant among the public works of art here is *Man* by **Alexander Calder**. In January, Montreal's **Winter Carnival** *(Fête des Neiges)* takes over the island *(see For Fun)*.
Also here are **The Old Fort and Stewart Museum★** *(see Historic Sites)*, the **Biosphère★** *(see Museums)* and **La Ronde★** amusement park *(See For Kids)*.

JEAN DRAPEAU PARK
Parc Jean-Drapeau

Île Ste-Hélène and Île Notre-Dame. Access via Pont de la Concorde (Concorde Bridge) or Pont Jacques-Cartier (Jacques Cartier Bridge). 514-872-6120. www.parcjeand rapeau.com. Open year-round daily 6am–midnight. Métro Jean-Drapeau, yellow line, then bus 167 around the park; or by bicycle or by boat from Jacques-Cartier Pier in the Old Port.

It's only a single subway stop from downtown but Jean Drapeau Park is, as they say, a world away. It hosted the entire world as the site

Island Sports
The pavements give way to the **Montreal F1 Grand Prix** automobile race in June, and the **NASCAR Busch Series** in August. At other times, the **Circuit Gilles-Villeneuve** track hums with inline skates. The **Olympic Basin** hosts rowing competitions.
www.grandprixmontreal.com

of the Expo '67 World's Fair, and Montrealers still enjoy the facilities left behind—the Biosphère, Montreal Casino, and La Ronde amusement park—to this day.

LA FONTAINE PARK
Parc La Fontaine

North of Rue Sherbrooke, between Ave. du Parc-La Fontaine & Ave. Papineau, and south of Rue Rachel. Open daily 6am–midnight. Métro Sherbrooke, orange line, or bus 24.

La Fontaine Park is an integral part of the urban fabric. Whereas the trails and paths of Mount Royal follow natural contours, the pavements of La Fontaine are geometrically inspired. While Mount Royal is largely wild, La Fontaine is planted to display colors throughout the milder months. Pedal boats are available for rental, Café Bistro Espace has reopened, and in winter, the pond becomes a skating rink. Cross-country skiers work out here, and the Théâtre de Verdure is Montreal's favorite outdoor performance venue. Most of the shows are free *(details at Centre Infotouriste; Dorchester Square, 1255 Rue Peel, or call 1-877-BONJOUR (266-5687); see Performing Arts)*.

🍁 BEST VIEWS

Montreal's topography encourages looking in all directions. Here are this island-city's must-view points, in parks, towers, and hidden aeries.

Mount Royal Park★★ – The forest in the city has two leading viewpoints. The **Chalet Lookout** *(Kondiaronk Belvédère)* reveals a fabulous **view★★★** of all of downtown, and the river and mountains beyond. **Camillien Houde Lookout** *(Belvédère Camillien-Houde)* features a **view★★** of the Port, Montreal Tower, & the east end.

Avenue McGill College – Gaze straight up one of the widest streets downtown, toward the greenery of McGill University, and beyond it, the forest of Mount Royal.

Montreal Tower – This 175m/574ft-tall leaning tower provides a thrill on the way up, and spectacular **views★★★** of the city from the top.

Port Panorama – Climb to the outside terrace of the **Pointe-à-Callière: Montreal Museum of Archaeology and History★★** *(350 Place Royale; see Museums)* for a view★ of the waterfront or head to the terrace bar atop the **Auberge du Vieux Port** *(97 Rue de la Commune Est)*. On Clock Tower pier, trek the 192 steps inside the **Clock Tower** itself.

Or climb the tower of the **Chapel of Our Lady of Good Help★** *(Chapelle Notre-Dame-de-Bon-Secours)* for the highest viewpoint accessible in Old Montreal *(see Historic Sites)*.

Revolving Courses – For dinner with an ever-changing outlook, head to the rooftop of **La Tour de Ville** restaurant at the Delta Centre-Ville Hotel *(777 Rue University; see Restaurants)*.

Westmount Summit Lookout – The mansions of one of the wealthiest neighborhoods in Canada are in the foreground of your **view★** to the St. Lawrence from the summit of Westmount *(take bus 166 on Chemin Côte-des-Neiges, then walk up Chemin Belvédère to Summit Circle)*.

View from Mount Royal

Old Montreal and Old Port

© Tourisme Montréal, Stéphan Poulin

Parc Jeanne-Mance *(north of Avenue des Pins, south of Avenue Mont-Royal)* – If travelers desire to people-watch the locals, this park has a bevy of dynamic sights and sounds. **Tam-Tam** every Sunday during fair weather, near the **Sir George-Etienne Cartier Monument**, is an unofficial gathering of souls who let loose on drums, dancing, singing, or playing instruments of their choice, or just watching. It's a great spot for **shopping** with inexpensive artisan collectibles, handmade clothing, and healthy snacks. Behind the gathering is a popular trail leading to the top of the mountain. It's also on a higher slope, so there's a good view of the surrounding neighborhood called **Le Plateau Mont-Royal**.

Parc Des Rapides *(Métro d'Église, then 58 bus west)* – This park is the best place to view the Island of Montreal as the early explorers had to traverse it, thundering **Lachine white-water rapids** included. Considered one of the six major parks, you will want to explore this 30ha/74-acre waterside haven of rare birds, enjoy a peaceful picnic, or simply watch this unique

spectacle. **Héritage Laurentien** naturalists are onsite to answer questions about wildlife, flora, and this magical place, which includes **Heron Island** and part of historic **Nun's Island** nearby.
Free parking.

Parc Cap Saint-Jacques *(at 288ha/721 acres)* – The largest park on the island is located at the far northwest tip in the neighborhood of Pierrefonds/Senneville. This park is a peninsula surrounded on three sides by water. Perched at the junction of the **Lake of Two Mountains** and **Rivière-des-Prairies**, residents of Montreal come here to visit the **beach**, working farm, walk or cycle through mixed maple and birch forests, or ski and snowshoe in winter. Take Trans Canada *(#40 highway)* west, then take the Ste-Marie exit west of Rue St-Charles and head west to the tiny mall, where you head north *(turn right)* on Rue L'Anse-a-L'Orme. At the "T" intersection at the end, head east *(turn right)* and continue for a short distance to the park's main entrance. *Cap-Saint-Jacques Nature Park 20099 Gouin Blvd. West Montreal 514-280-PARC.*

BEST VIEWS

75

QUEBEC CITY★★★

Don't think of Quebec City as only a provincial capital. It's the spiritual home of one of Canada's two founding peoples, a fortress of national identity as well as a fortified city. Quebec City perches on a high point at a narrows—"kebec" in the Algonquian Amerindian language— where the St. Charles River flows into the St. Lawrence. Explorer Jacques Cartier landed here in 1535, and Samuel de Champlain set up a fur-trading post in 1608.

Today Nouvelle France is alive within the old city walls, fieldstone buildings with steeply pitched roofs, and narrow, winding streets. The battlefield of the Plains of Abraham recalls what's still known as *La Defaite* (The Defeat) by French Canadians. Indeed, Quebec City embodies a resolve to preserve, protect, and develop the major French-speaking society in the Western Hemisphere. Sophisticated Quebec City claims fine hotels, cutting-edge restaurants, a celebration of winter pleasures, and nearby ski resorts that make it a lively destination 365 days a year. Come in winter to experience the city shining against a carpet of snow, in spring or summer when flowers bloom alongside stone ramparts, or in fall when the countryside glows in shades of red and gold.

POPULATION

Prior to the Conquest, the town's population was made up of French settlers. The influx of British and Irish immigrants in the early 19C led to an increase in the Anglophone population, which numbered 41 percent in 1851, and reached 51 percent by 1861. Following Quebec City's economic decline, the population shift westward decreased the number of Anglophones to 31.5 percent in 1871, and 10 percent in 1921. In 2006, Anglophones accounted for just 1.66 percent of Quebec City's residents, thereby affirming the city's distinct Francophone character.

QUEBEC CITY TODAY

Throughout the centuries, Quebec City has retained its role as a capital city and as a bastion of French culture. The colonial French city is much more in evidence here than in Montreal. In the last three decades, the growth of the provincial government has given the city a new boost, and a bustling metropolis has developed outside the old walls. In contrast to the modern cities of North America, Quebec City has retained a cachet reminiscent of Old World capitals. The city's main event is its famous winter **Carnival**. Held in February, this festival attracts thousands of visitors. For 10 joyous days, Quebec City bustles with festivities that include a daily parade, the construction of a magnificent ice palace, an international ice sculpture contest, and canoe races over the partially frozen St. Lawrence. The activities are overseen by an enormous snowman, nicknamed *Bonhomme Carnaval*.

NEIGHBORHOODS

...ure, there are ethnic enclaves like Chinatown and Little Italy, but ...ontreal's quartiers have twists you'll rarely find in North America. ...avel back in time by strolling into Old Montreal, or explore public ...quares that are indoors. Find chic creations on Rue Saint-Denis and ...eek fashions in Outremont. You'll even encounter Westmount, ...here the English-speakers are a quaint ethnic group with their ...wn peculiar customs. Vive la différence!

...ASSE-VILLE★★★ ...LOWER TOWN)

...e Lower Town began in the ...rly 17C as a fur-trading post, ...tablished by Champlain on ...e area around his "Habitation." ...1636, the year following de ...hamplain's death, the first city ...ans were drawn up. Between ...50 and 1662, more than 35 ...arcels of land were conceded ...merchants, who began ...nstructing shops and residences ...ound the Habitation and its ...djoining square, then called the ...arket Place (place du marché). ...mited space in the Lower Town ...spired the residents to fill in ...arts of the shore northeast of the ...uare and erect wharves along ...e Saint-Pierre.

...August 1682 a fire devastated ...e Lower Town. As a result of ...is disaster, building standards, ...ch as the use of stone rather ...an wood, were imposed on new ...nstructions, giving rise to the ...mple stone box construction ...sible throughout the quarter ...day. As commerce, shipbuilding, ...d port activities grew in the 19C, ...e area occupied by the Lower ...wn doubled in size. Port activity ...clined after 1860, severing the ...onomic lifeline of the Lower ...wn and resulting in progressive ...terioration of the buildings in the

area over the next century. In 1967 the Quebec Government passed legislation to support restoration of Place Royale. The archaeological and restoration work began in 1970 and continues today. The Lower Town's commercial vocation still marks the area, as evidenced in the market squares, wharves, and warehouses.

HAUTE-VILLE★★★ (UPPER TOWN)

Originally described as an "inhospitable rock, permanently unfit for habitation," the massive Cap Diamant (named that way because it resembles the shape of a rough diamond) was the site of Champlain's strategic Fort Saint-Louis (1620), built in the center of a staked enclosure. Enlarged in 1629 and renamed Château Saint-Louis, the modest wood structure was replaced by a single-story building in 1692. At the request of the Count of Frontenac, it became the official residence of the governor of the colony. Rebuilt after sustaining severe damage during the Conquest, the edifice was razed by fire in 1834. The Upper Town was not developed until a group of wealthy merchants, the Company of One Hundred Associates (Compagnie des Cent-Associés), decided to increase settlement in the colony.

NEIGHBORHOODS

The land belonging to a handful of seigneurs was redistributed, and the parcels owned by religious institutions were reduced.

The first efforts to urbanize the Upper Town were initiated under Governor Montmagny's administration (1636–48). Though constrained by the hilly topography of the site, as well as the presence of vast lands belonging to institutions, Montmagny planned to erect a large, fortified city. The first houses appeared toward the end of the 17C, near the Place d'Armes and along Rue Saint-Louis. However, the Ursuline, Augustine, and Jesuit orders long refused to divide up their land plots, and the military opposed the construction of buildings near fortifications, thus halting any rapid development of the town. By the late 18C, the buildings still reflected the administrative and religious presence in the district.

During the 19C, a new residential neighborhood evolved along Rues Saint-Louis, Sainte-Ursule, and d'Auteuil, and Avenues Sainte-Geneviève and Saint-Denis, only to be surpassed in 1880, by the Grande Allée, sometimes known as the "Champs Élysées" of Quebec City. Today, the Upper Town forms the heart of Old Quebec (Vieux-Québec), and still functions as the city's administrative center.

GRANDE ALLÉE★

Departing from the St. Louis gate and extending southward of Old Quebec, the Grande Allée is the city's Champs-Élysées. Lined with an abundance of restaurants, bars, outdoor cafes, boutiques, and offices, Quebec City's premier thoroughfare provides an elegant setting for the city's nightlife. Grande Allée developed along the east-west axis that separated the land plots allotted to a few major property holders on the Quebec plateau in the early 17C. Originally a country road, it acquired a sudden popularity in the late 18C, when it was transformed into a resort district by the British. In just a few years, magnificent villas appeared along the south side of Grande Allée, and the Faubourg Saint-Louis began taking shape. Adding to the shift of business activity to Montreal and the move of the Canadian Parliament to Ottawa, the departure of the British garrison in 1871 hastened the decline of Quebec City. Inspired by the new city of Edinburgh, which developed alongside the original medieval town, the municipal engineer Charles Baillairgé suggested Grande Allée be transformed into one of Quebec City's main arteries. A fire destroyed the Faubourg Saint-Louis on July 1, 1876, clearing much of the area and prompting the decision to erect the Parliament Building on this site. Following construction in 1886, the boulevard was designed as a corridor for official procession linking the Parliament Building to Bois-de-Coulonge Park, the official residence of the lieutenant governor.

The first residents of the remodeled Grande Allée (1886–90) were the political elite of the city, who built opulent villas in the Second Empire style. Between 1890 and 1900, the upper portion of the boulevard was further developed with the arrival

f a new bourgeoisie reaping
he benefits of the Lower Town's
industrialization. The heyday of
Grande Allée continued well after
World War I, and came to an end
with the opening of the Quebec
ity Bridge to cars in 1929, which
ransformed the residential district
into a busy thoroughfare.

FORTIFICATIONS★★

In the 17C, Quebec City played
key role in the defense of
northeastern French America. As a
onsequence of the city's strategic
ocation, several fortification
rojects were undertaken over the
ears. However, the construction of
atteries, redoubts, and cavaliers in
oth the Lower and Upper towns
eased following the signing of
he Utrecht Treaty of 1713, which
emporarily suspended hostilities
etween the European factions.
During the ensuing peace,
eripheral forts were the most
ommon means of defense.
The fortification of Quebec City
esumed in 1745 in reaction to
he capture of Louisbourg, on the
land of Cape Breton in present-
ay Nova Scotia. French military
ngineer Gaspard Chaussegros de
éry initiated the new fortification
roject, which was completed
y the British after the Conquest
f 1759. The British erected a
emporary citadel in 1783, then
dded four circular Martello towers
(1805–12), and finally built a new,
ermanent citadel between 1820
nd 1832. The fortifications were
aced with red sandstone from a
ap-Rouge quarry.
ollowing the departure of the
ritish garrison in 1871, local
ilitary authorities approved the

demolition of certain city gates
to facilitate passage between
the Lower and Upper towns and
the Saint-Jean and Saint-Louis
faubourgs. Influenced by the
Romantic movement then popular
in Europe, Lord Dufferin, governor-
general of Canada from 1872 to
1878, insisted on the preservation
of Quebec's fortifications.
In 1875, he submitted a plan for
the beautification of Quebec City,
which included refurbishing the
fortified enceinte, rebuilding the
gates to the city, and demolishing
all the advanced military works
that formed a 60m/200ft wide strip
along the ramparts, in order to fully
expose the complex in the manner
of medieval fortifications.
As a result of Lord Dufferin's
initiative, visitors can now stroll
along the fortification walkways
and enjoy panoramic **views**.

LA CITADELLE

This instalment is unique in North
America. After all, this is the only
fortified city north of Mexico.
The star-shaped Citadel, built by
the British to protect themselves
against attack by the Americans,
took over 30 years to construct.
Ceremonies such as **The Beating
of Retreat** and **Changing of the
Guard** are recreated for tourists in
summertime on this beautiful
Cape Diamond locale. The Citadel
is still actively used by the **Royal
22nd Regiment** of the Canadian
Army, known worldwide as the
Van Doos. The **Musée du Royal
22nd Regiment** has an irresistible
collection of military paperwork,
armaments, wardrobe, and artifacts
covering 400 years of military life in
North America. This is one-of-a-kind.

NEIGHBORHOODS

LOWER TOWN★★★

Follow Rue du Petit-Champlain down from the ramparts of Quebec City to a 19C seaport. What began as a trading post was taken over by English merchants, who erected their banks, warehouses, and docks along the waterside. The solid bones of those old buildings have in many cases been recycled into the charming hotels of today. Begin the tour at Rue du Petit-Champlain (2.2km/1.4mi).

Maison Louis-Jolliet
Louis-Jolliet House

16 Rue du Petit-Champlain. Open daily 7.30am–11.30pm, $2, 418-692-1132. www.funiculaire-Quebec.com.

Constructed by architect/stonemason Claude Bailiff in 1693 for the first Quebec-born resident to make history. Louis Jolliet was a cartographer, fur trader, and co-discoverer of the Mississippi River with Father Jacques Marquette. This house was base camp for him and his fellow explorers on their westward treks. He was the first European to see the Mississippi and first to make a detailed map. His house became the entry point for visitors riding the world-famous Funiculaire from 1879. This 60m (200ft) long cable car ride brings visitors up the escarpment at a 45-degree pitch. One of the most unique attractions in the city, and a great place to snap photos of the port, Château Frontenac, and Lower Town.

Économusée: Richard Robitaille Fourrers

329 Rue Saint-Paul. Open year-round Mon–Sat 9.30am–4pm, Bus #1. 418-692-9699. www.economusee.com.

A cross-pollination between a workshop and museum, here you

Cable Car

A funicular (cable car) also connects Dufferin Terrace (in front of Château Frontenac) to the Lower Town *(in service year-round, daily 7.30am–11.30pm; $1.75; 418-692-1132; www.funiculaire-quebec.com).*

will find Serge Richard and other artisans designing and repairing furs of many species. Watch the tradition of piecing together a full-length fur coat. See the unique tools and workflow techniques handed down since the beaver pelts ruled New France and were the rage across Europe in the 1600s and 1700s.

Marvel at hat-making molds, scales antique sewing machines, and a rich onsite source of information on numerous animals and hunting techniques serving this industry. Boutique shop for authentic (and cozy!) souvenirs.

Quartier Petit-Champlain★

50 shops open Mon–Wed 9.30am–5.30pm, Thu/Fri until 9pm, Sat/Sun 9.30am–5pm. Check for showtimes and live music venues. www.quartierpetitchamplain.com.

Even non-shoppers will love this romantic pedestrian thoroughfare at the base of the escarpment,

Quartier Petit Champlain

©Claudel Huot

deemed the "oldest commercial district in North America." Open throughout the year, this non-traffic stretch is a visual joy after fresh snowfall.

Maison Chevalier★
(Chevalier House)

50 Rue du Marché-Champlain, on Place Royale. Open Jun 24–Labor Day, daily 9.30am–5.30pm; rest of the year, Tue–Sun 10am–5pm. Audio & guided tours available. 418-646-3167 & 1-866-710-8031. www.mcq.org.

One of busiest buildings of the late-18C occupies the site of the **Cul-de-Sac**, a natural port discovered by Champlain. It was so busy here, stonemasons had to round rocks at the corner of the structure so carriages could more easily make the turn. The King's shipyards, originally established at the mouth of the St. Charles River, were moved here in 1745 but the basin was filled in during the mid-18C in an effort to enlarge the area of Lower Town.

Formerly the London Coffee House, this crimson-roof structure

underneath Château Frontenac. Known as Rue De Meulles in the 1690s, early wooden and stone dwellings have been lovingly refurbished and now offer one-of-a-kind art galleries, typical Quebec bistros, cafes, artisan boutiques, and there's even a live performance theater and quaint park. Several generations of restoration work carried out by a joint public and private effort has transformed the entire street into a festive district

Maison Chevalier

is composed of three separate buildings. A wing was added in 1752 for the wealthy merchant and shipowner, Jean-Baptiste Chevalier. The house was then destroyed by fire in 1762. Acquired by the Quebec Government in 1956 as part of the Museum of Civilization, the Chevalier House was further dressed up to present exhibits on traditional Quebec architecture and furniture. Continue to the corner of Rue du Marché-Champlain and Boulevard Champlain to enjoy the superb **view★** of the imposing Château Frontenac, looming over the Lower Town.

▷ *Return to the Chevalier House; turn right on Rue Notre-Dame and right on Rue Sous-le-Fort.*

Batterie Royale
(Royal Battery)

Rampart at the end of Rue Sous-le-Fort and Rue Saint-Pierre.

Constructed in 1690 to fend off the English at the request of Louis XIV, King of France, this thick, four-sided earthen rampart formed part of the fortifications designed to strengthen Quebec. Immediately beside the river, the battery suffered from the extreme winters and was frequently in a state of disrepair. All but destroyed during the Conquest, the defense was not rebuilt. Instead, the British erected two warehouses and a wharf on the site. The Royal Battery went subterranean until two centuries later, when archaeologists unearthed it in 1972. Today, this historic rampart has been reconstructed, and replicas of 18C cannons are positioned in embrasures. Originally designed

by architect Claude Bailiff and engineer Franquelin, from June to Labor Day historical re-enactments and interpretive demonstrations on the operation of the cannons take place. Children are particularly fascinated by the perils soldiers faced operating those huge guns.

▷ *Turn right on Rue Saint-Pierre, then left on Ruelle de la Place, which leads to Place Royale.*

Place Royale★★
Bounded by Rue Notre-Dame & Rue St-Pierre between Rue Sous-le-Fort & Rue du Porche.
The main square of Lower Town, cobblestone Place Royale was the site of the settlement's early market. On the north side of the square, you'll find a sculpture of Louis XIV of France; it's a copy of a marble sculpture made in 1665 by Bernini. Flanking the south side of the square, the **Church of Our Lady of Victories★** (Église Notre-Dame-des-

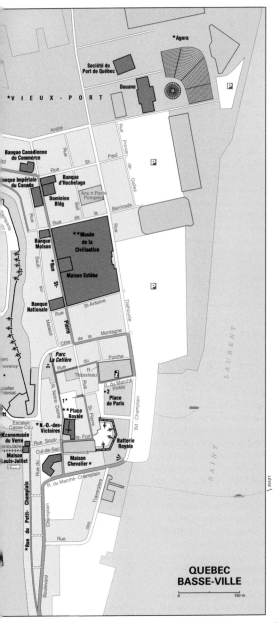

★ Agora

Société du
Port de Québec

Douane

★ V I E U X - P O R T

André

Rue St-Paul

Rue Princes de Galles

Banque Canadienne
de Commerce

Rue St-

Banque Imperiale
du Canada

Banque
d'Hochelaga

Anc.n Poste
Pompiers

Dominion
Bldg

bd de la Barricade

Rue de la Rue

Banque
Molson

Rue St-
Saub-
aur

★★ Musée
de la
Civilisation

Maison Estèbe

Banque
Nationale

Rue
Pierre

Matelot

St-Antoine

L. Dalhousie

Côte de la Montagne

Parc
La Cetière

R. Notre-Dame

Rue
du
R. Thibodeau

Porche

R. du Marché-
Finlay

i

norency

calier
tenac

1 ·
★★ Place
Royale

Place
de Paris

Rue St-Pierre

Bd Champlain

Escalier
Casse-Cou

★ N.-D.-des-
Victoires

·2

Économusée
du Verre

Rue Sous-

le-Fort

Batterie
Royale

aniculaire
Maison
Louis-Jollet

Maison
Chevalier ★

Rue du

Cul-de-Sac

R. du Marché- Champlain

Traversière

★ Rue du Petit- Champlain

Champlain

Rue

Boulevard

L A U R E N T

S A I N T

QUEBEC
BASSE-VILLE

0   150 m

Victoires) commemorates two early successes against the English. It was built between 1688 and 1723 as an auxilliary chapel to Quebec's main cathedral to serve the congregation in Lower Town. Running along the east side of Place Royale, **Rue Saint-Pierre★** was the main business street of Quebec City in the 19C, home to the first insurance company in Canada, as well as banks and trading companies. Many of its buildings are wonderfully preserved. If you continue left on **Rue Saint-Paul★**, with its boutiques and restaurants housed in centuries-old brick buildings, you'll soon arrive at the **Old Port★** *(Vieux-Port)*.

Église Notre-Dame-des-Victoires★
(Church of Our Lady of the Victories)

32 Rue Sous-le-Fort. Open May–mid-Oct, 9.30am–5pm; rest of the year, Mon–Sat 10am–4pm. Guided tours in French and English. 418-692-1650 & 418-692-2533.

Built between 1688 and 1723, this captivationg locale has quite a history, and is the exact site for Champlain's "Habitation." Built as an auxiliary chapel of Basilica Notre-Dame, it served their congregation in Lower Town. Completely trashed by cannon balls during the Battle of the Plains of Abraham in 1759, it went on to become a police station, monastery, and even home to the national lottery. Stunning frescoes adorn the choir recalling these victories: 1690, when Admiral Phips' fleet was defeated by the troops of the Count de Frontenac, and again in 1711, when Admiral

Walker's fleet was shipwrecked during a storm. A handmade model of the ship *Brézé*, a transport vessel for French troops, hangs curiously in the nave, while the original 1729 organ, destroyed in 1759 and later rebuilt several times by Barker (1870), Abbey (1898), and Kern (1972) can be heard at local baptisms and weddings.

▷ *Leave Place Royale by Rue Notre-Dame.*

Parc La Cetière
(La Cetière Park)

The gigantic Fresque des Québeçois (Mural of Quebecers) colorfully depicts historical moments here, while overlooking an archaeological dig first shoveled in 1972. Stone underpinnings of the original dwellings date back to 1685. Destroyed during the Conquest, all five stone houses from this block were rebuilt on the same foundations.

▷ *Take Rue du Porche and turn right on Rue Thibaudeau.*

Place de Paris

An ideal vantage point for historical features of amazing Old World structures; chimneysweep ladders afixed to rooftops, beautifully shuttered windows, stonecutter's virtuosity everywhere you look. Once the St. Lawrence River shoreline spot where the prosperous Finlay Market (1817) stood, today a contemporary sculpture entitled *Dialogue with History* marks the center of the vast, open square. A gift from the city of Paris, it was designed to commemorate the landing of the first French settlers. The **Centre d'Interpretation de Place Royale** *(27 Rue Notre-Dame; open Jun 24– Labor Day, daily 9.30am–5pm; rest of the year, Tue–Sun 10am–5pm; $6; 418-646-3167; www.mcq.org)* is a successful example of doing more with less, and a Must-See classic. Newest member of the Museum of Civilization group, objects recovered from archaeological digs beneath the square bear witness to 400 years of history. **Facing Champlain: A Work in 3 Dimensions** brings multimedia 3-D presentations to a new high, while the **Hands-On Room** allows vistors to peak inside early French-Canadian life.

◗ *Leave the square by turning left on Rue Dalhousie, then turn left on Côte de la Montagne and right on Rue Saint-Pierre.*

Rue Saint-Pierre★

During the 19C, this road was dubbed the Wall Street of Quebec. Now there are fortunes hanging on the walls of numerous galleries representing au courant (cool)

Quebec painters, sculptors, jewelry designers, and multimedia artists. Banks, insurance companies, and the Stock Exchange established HQs on this street and have now become boutique hotels, eateries, and spas. A good example is the **Dominion Building** *(no. 126, and now the popular Hotel Germain)*, Quebec City's first skyscraper. Just around the corner is the city's amazing **Museum of Civilization**.

Museum of Civilization★★
Musée de la Civilisation

85 Rue Dalhousie. Open year-round Tue–Sun 10am–5pm. $13. 418-643-2158. www.mcq.org.

With all the civilization embodied in the buildings and culture of the Upper Town, a museum in the Lower Town had better be good! And it is.
The Museum of Civilization is architect Moshe Safdie's modern interpretation of Quebec's temples of old. Natural light floods down into exhibition spaces, while steep roof lines reflect those of the old city.

Museum of Civilization

Cidra Labrie/Musée de la civilisation

LOWER TOWN: WALKING TOUR

This is not quite an art museum, though it has paintings and sculptures. It's not a history or natural history museum either, though it displays artifacts from cultures around the world, especially those of Quebec's Inuit and First Nations peoples.

It's not an ethnology museum, though it exhibits costumes, and not a kids' museum, though there are always hands-on exhibitions. Altogether, it's a museum dedicated to being in touch with the human adventure here and everywhere, in the past, present, and future.

Vieux-Port★
(Old Port)

Access at the corner of Rues Dalhousie and Saint-André. 418-648-3640.

Covering an area of 33ha/81.5 acres, the port installations are located around the Pointe-à-Carcy, where the St. Charles River joins the St. Lawrence. From the settlement of the colony until the mid-19C, the port played a major role in the development of Canada. Imported goods, exported furs and timber, and thousands of immigrants passed through this harbor. Activity declined in the second half of the 19C when the port fell into disrepair.

In the mid-1980s, a revitalization project financed by the federal government changed the face of the old port with the creation of the **Agora★** complex, which includes an open-air amphitheater built between the St. Lawrence River and the Customs House, and a wide boardwalk along the river. A marina for several hundred pleasure boats complements the former maritime hub, plus the mammoth **Café du Monde** eatery, where politicians, sailors, and travelers dine shoulder-to-shoulder overlooking the port.

Édifice de la Douane
(Customs House)

2 Rue Saint-André.

Overlooking the St. Lawrence, the majestic Neoclassical structure (1856–60) was designed by the English architect, William Thomas. Cut stone masks and masonry dressing ornament the ground-floor windows.

Fire ravaged the interior of the Customs House in 1864 and again in 1909, destroying the upper level and the dome.

The door knocker on the main entrance originally hung on the first English Customs House established in Quebec City in 1793. The building was completely restored between 1979 and 1981, and is still occupied by the administrative offices of the Customs Service. Today it is known as one of Quebec's most beautiful buildings and is part of the city's identity.

Société du Port de Québec
(Port of Quebec Building)

Rue Saint-André. www.portquébec.ca.

Designed by local architect Thomas R. Peacock, the building (1914) stands on the site where, in 1909, a fire destroyed a grain elevator and also damaged the Customs House.

UPPER TOWN★★★

The narrow, winding streets, massive stone walls, turrets, and crenellations and gateways of Quebec City create a fairy-tale setting. It's all real, a living city where people come to work and shop, as well as relax and have fun and experience the joie de vivre of the Old Capital. It's Old Europe, with fieldstone buildings hugging each other close to the street. But it's also the new, with Quebec's signature steep roofs to shed the snow loads. Wander at will in Quebec City's Upper Town. You won't run out of things to see, historical buildings to enchant you, lanes to follow, crannies to peek into, and cafes where you can sip an apéritif. Begin the tour at Place d'Armes *(2km/1.2mi)*.

Place d'Armes★★

From the St. Louis Gate on the Grande Allée, head all the way down Rue St-Louis to the main square of the old city. Once a parade and exercise ground for the troops of His Majesty the King of France, 100 years ago it became a public green space. In the center is

Château View

The prominence of *Château Frontenac* in the city's landscape can be best appreciated from high atop the citadel, from the Marie-Guyart Building observatory, or from the Lévis terrace.

the **Monument to Faith** *(Monument de la Foi)*, a 1916 sculpture that recalls the arrival of the first priest to Quebec City in 1615.

Le Château Frontenac★★

1 Rue des Carrières. 418-692-3861. www.fairmont.ca. See Hotels: Quebec City.

A hotel is a hotel, except when it's also a castle, and the most visible landmark of a city. Opened in 1893 by the Canadian Pacific Railway, the Château Frontenac takes its inspiration from the styles popular in Quebec City at the time, which in turn were inspired by the châteaux

Le Château Frontenac

©Juliane Martini/Michelin

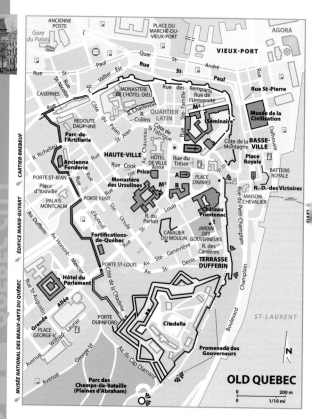

Map labels (Old Quebec):

ANCIENNE POSTE · PLACE DU MARCHÉ-DU-VIEUX-PORT · AGORA · Gare du Palais · VIEUX-PORT · Quai St-André · Rue St-Paul · Rue St-Vallier Est · Rue St-Nicolas · CASERNES · MONASTÈRE DE L'HÔTEL-DIEU · Rue des Remparts · Rue de l'Université · Rue St-Pierre · Rue St-Paul · QUARTIER LATIN · Rue Ste-Famille · Rue St-Jean · Côte du Palais · R. Charlevoix · R. Collins · Séminaire · Musée de la Civilisation · Dalhousie · REDOUTE DAUPHINE · Parc-de-l'Artillerie · Côte de la Fabrique · Côte de la Montagne · BASSE-VILLE · Ancienne Fonderie · HAUTE-VILLE · Rue Cook · HÔTEL DE VILLE · Rue du Trésor · Place Royale · R. Richelieu · Av. Chauveau · Rue Ste-Anne · BATTERIE ROYALE · PORTE ST-JEAN · Price · Monastère des Ursulines · PLACE D'ARMES · N.-D.-des-Victoires · Place d'Youville · PORTE KENT · R. du Parloir · Rue St-Louis · MAISON CHEVALIER · PALAIS MONTCALM · d'Auteuil · Ste-Ursule · Château Frontenac · JARDIN DES GOUVERNEURS · R. des Carrières · Fortifications-de-Québec · CAVALIER DU MOULIN · Ste-Geneviève · TERRASSE DUFFERIN · PORTE ST-LOUIS · Av. Ste-Denis · Hôtel du Parlement · Côte de la Citadelle · ST-LAURENT · Grande Allée · PLACE GEORGE-V · Av. Wilfrid Laurier · Av. George-VI · PORTE DURNFORD · Citadelle · Promenade des Gouverneurs · Boulevard Champlain · Av. du Cap-Diamant · Parc des Champs-de-Bataille (Plaines d'Abraham) · OLD QUEBEC · N · 0 — 200 m · 0 — 1/10 mi

Side margins: CARTIER-BRÉBEUF · ÉDIFICE MARIE-GUYART · MUSÉE NATIONAL DES BEAUX-ARTS DU QUÉBEC · LÉVIS

---

of France. Like a true castle, the Château Frontenac winds in several wings around a central courtyard, its brick and stone walls capped by steep copper roofs. In its day, the Château came to embody the brand image of the railway and it was imitated to some degree—but never duplicated—in railway cities across Canada.

Try to spot the rooster claws on the facade above the coach gate—coat-of-arms of the Count of Frontenac, once governor of New France. Inside the courtyard you'll find a stone relief of the Maltese Cross, taken from the residence of another governor.

○ *Continue along Rue Saint-Louis.*

Ancien Palais de Justice★
(Old Courthouse)

12 Rue Saint-Louis.

Now housing the Ministry of Finance, this Second Empire-style building (1887) was erected on the site of the former Récollet convent and church, both destroyed by fire during the late 18C. The facades were fashioned after 16C Loire Valley châteaux. On each side of the main entrance, notice the rare coats-of-arms of explorers Jacques Cartier and Samuel de Champlain. You see their names everywhere, but these familial icons are singular.

Maison Maillou★
(Maillou House) (A)

17 Rue Saint-Louis.

Next door neighbor to Château Frontenac, this fieldstone address boasts a steeply-pitched copper roof and hides a large inner courtyard. A good example of a building which has been "Canadianized," using high-quality materials matched with traditional stylings, it was built c.1736 by the architect Jean Maillou (1668–1753). Enlarged in 1799, the house was once occupied by the British Army and the exterior metal shutters on the windows date from this period. Carefully restored in 1964, the Maillou House is typical of the 1800s home of the French settlers. The immediate neighborhoods includes no. 25, the offices of the Consulate General of France, who occupy the former **Maison Kent** (Kent House) (**B**). Dating back to the 18C, this large white structure adorned with bright blue trim was rebuilt in the 1830s. The Duke of Kent, father of Queen Victoria, called this home from 1792–94.

Maison Jacquet★
(Jacquet House) (C)

34 Rue Saint-Louis.

Accepted as the oldest house in Quebec City, this one-story structure, topped by a steep red roof, was erected on land acquired

from the Ursuline Nuns in 1674. Author Philippe Aubert de Gaspé lived here from 1815–24, giving the house its current name, Maison des Anciens Canadiens (Home of the Early Canadians), from the title of his 1863 novel. Today a popular restaurant, it is arguably the most authentic place in the province to sample traditional Québécois cuisine, like Lac Saint-Jean meat pie (aka tourtiére), maple sugar on bread, or Matane shrimp. The busy reservation book atests to this dining room's prowess. Try eating an all-inclusive lunchtime table d'hôte (soup/salad, main course, and dessert) as dinner is much more expensive.

○ *Turn right onto Rue des Jardins and left onto Rue Donnacona.*

Ursuline Monastery★★
Monastère des Ursulines

6 Rue Donnacona. Chapel: 418-694-0413. Open June–Oct Tue–Sat 10am–11.30am & 1.30pm–4.30pm, Sun 1pm–5pm. Museum: 418-694-0694. $6. Open May–Sept Tue–Sat 10am–noon & 1pm–5pm, Sun 1pm–5pm; closed Nov–June.

Talk about Old School—this is the oldest women's school in the hemisphere, and it's still going strong. Started in 1641, it has outlasted fires, conquest, and renovations, all the while maintaining its extensive gardens and orchard. The **chapel** dates from early in the 20C, and has an inner sanctum restricted to use by nuns of the order. The sculptures and other fine **ornamentation**★★ largely come from earlier constructions—many pieces were gilded by the sisters themselves. The **museum**★★ in an adjacent house at no. 12 recalls the everyday life of the order through furnishings and documents. See their permanent exhibition on girls' education.

◗ *Return to Rue Saint Louis by Rue du Parloir and turn right.*
Across from no. 58, on Rue du Corps-de-Garde, check out the cannonball exposed in the roots of a tree. The wall of the Cavalier du Moulin park rises in the background. At no. 72, a plaque reminds any General Montgomery fans of his failed attack on Quebec City by American forces in 1775.

◗ *Turn left on Rue Sainte-Ursule and pass the Église Unie Saint-Pierre (Chalmers-Wesley United Church), whose Gothic-revival structure is shared by two Protestant congregations, one Francophone, the other Anglophone.*

◗ *Backtrack on Rue Sainte-Ursule past Rue Saint-Louis.*

Ursuline Monastery

On the northwest corner of Rues Saint-Louis and Sainte-Ursule stood the first city hall of Quebec City, founded in 1833. When the present City Hall opened in 1896, combining offices for the city under one roof, row houses were erected along Rue Sainte-Ursule (*nos. 60–68*), creating a mixed-use ambiance to the street.

◗ *Continue to the intersection with Rue Sainte-Anne, turn right, and continue to the intersection with Rue Cook.*

St. Andrew's Presbyterian Church

106 Rue Sainte-Anne. Open Jul–Aug, Mon–Fri 10am–4pm. Bilingual guided tours. On Sundays, English mass at 10.30am. 418-694-1347. www.standrewsquebec.ca.

This is the oldest English-speaking congregation of Scottish origin in Canada. Hoots mon!
Built in 1810 for Presbyterian Scots in Quebec City, the church was enlarged in 1823. The distinctive sounds of their legendary Pipes and Drums Corps can be heard in rehearsals.

◗ *Continue along Rue Sainte-Anne.*

Price Building★

65 Rue Sainte-Anne.

Not everything in the Upper Town is as old as the Conquest. Quebec City's first skyscraper, dating from 1930, rose to all of 16 storys in Art-Deco style, with decorative elements—squirrels, pine cones—that made it unabashedly Canadian; unusual for its day.

© Tibor Bognar/Age Fotostock

Hotel Clarendon

57 Rue Sainte-Anne. 418-692-2480.
www.hotelclarendon.com.

In 1943, Churchill and Roosevelt met here for two weeks to plan the Normandy Invasion for WWII. Now one of Canada's venerable jazz clubs onsite provides listeners with the rare continuity of weekly live jazz. The original builder of this Art-Deco structure, Charles Baillairgé, erected two houses here for a printer named Desbarats in 1870. The property was converted into a hotel in 1875.

Anglican Cathedral of the Holy Trinity★
La Cathédrale Holy Trinity

31 Rue des Jardins. Morning prayers weekdays 8.30am, Thu noon Eucharist, Sun Choral English 11.00am. 418-692-2193. Gift shop open 10am–4pm in summer.

King George III himself paid for the construction of this first Anglican cathedral outside the British Isles, opening in 1804. The famous church bells rang here in 1830 for the very first time, and if you've been to London, you'll recognize the similarity to St. Martin in the Fields, although the roof had to be raised on this Neoclassical Palladian example to accommodate heavy winter snows.

Information Touristique

12 Rue Sainte-Anne.
Open throughout the year from 9am. 418-694-2001.
www.bonjourQuebec.com.

Facing the Place d'Armes, this large structure (1805–12) exemplifies Palladian-style architectecture. It used to be the Union Hotel and now provides info and tours as the government's regional tourist kiosk. Ask about their **Ghost Lantern Walk**, **whale tours**, and **SEPAQ national park access**.

Musée du Fort★
(Fort Museum) (M4)

10 Rue Sainte-Anne. Open Feb–Mar & Nov, Thu–Sun 11am–4pm; Apr–Oct, daily 10am–5pm. $8. 418-692-2175. http://museedufort.com.

Erected in 1840, this square white building topped by a grey roof was modified in 1898, giving it a whimsical appearance. An excellently narrated sound and light presentation (*30min*) cast upon a large-scale model of Quebec during the 18C traces the city's military and civil history from its foundation in 1608 until the American invasion of 1775–76. The maquette itself provides a unique perspective of the city's distinctive topography.

◗ *Turn left on Rue du Fort and continue to Rue Buade.*

Ancien Bureau de Poste
(Old Post Office) (D)

Entrance at 3 Passage du Chien-D'Or, near Dufferin Terrace. Open early Jul–early Oct, Mon–Fri 10am–6pm. Closed major holidays. Entrance fee and guided tours to Fort Saint-Louis and Châteaux NHS. 418-648-7016. parkscanada.gc.ca/ca/ saintlouis.

Beaux-Arts embellishments highlight this 1873 former post office. Hand-cut stone leads the design features, while its original size was doubled in 1914. Until

1837, an inn called Chien-D'Or (Golden Dog) occupied the site and if you look closely, you can still see the bas-relief advertising the inn above the entrance.

Renamed to honor former Canadian Prime Minister, the Louis S. St-Laurent Building still operates as a working post office. A new archeological National Historic Site operated by Canadian Parks Service presents period costumed guides revealing details of life and this first seat of power during the 16C.

Monsignor de Laval Monument (2)

The city fathers went all out to celebrate the bicentennial of the death of this first bishop of New France, leveling a whole city block of houses. The final sculpting was designed by Louis-Philippe Hébert and positioned in front of the old post office. We can thank François de Montmorency-Laval (1623–1708) for the generous square created in his name.

Rue Buade ends at the **Charles-Baillairgé Stairway** (1893), named in honor of the Quebec City architect. He came from a local family filled with artists and architects, was a noted author (publishing over 250 books) and was the first managing architect for Canada's first Parliament Buildings in Ottawa, as well as Laval University here.

◐ *Descend the stairs and continue up Côte de la Montagne.*

From the foot of the stairs, note the monumental false front of the old post office dominating the Lower Town.

Palais Archiépiscopal (Archbishop's Palace) (E)

2 Rue Port-Dauphin.

Wonderfully placed at the heights of the Upper Town, this Neoclassical palace was constructed in the late 17C in Montmorency Park, then re-done in 1847. As part of Lord Dufferin's beautification projects, a phony facade was raised, looking toward the Côte de la Montagne, and allowing the building to be visible from the St. Lawrence River. This original frontispiece is hard to miss in the main courtyard, where it leads visitors to the old seminary.

◐ *Return to Rue Buade.*

Facing the Beaux-Arts style presbytery *(16 Rue Buade at the corner of Rue du Fort)*, a plaque draws attention to the foundations of a funeral chapel thought to contain the tomb of master mariner **Samuel de Champlain**. Of course there are numerous theories about the final resting place for the **Father of New France**, but this location is top of the experts' list.

Basilique-Cathédrale Notre-Dame-de-Québec★ (Basilica-Cathedral of Our Lady of Quebec)

20 Rue De Baude, at Côte de la Fabrique. Opening hours vary by season. Guided tours $3 (French and English), plus many events year round: Check calendar on website. 418-694-0665. www.patrimoine-religieux.com.

The oldest parish in North America, this was declared a historical

Basilique Notre-Dame-de-Québec

©Doug Rogers/MICHELIN

World Heritage Site. Walk into the attached park, Place de l' Hôtel-de-Ville, to the Taschereau Monument, first Cardinal in Canada), where two important trails begin: Route de la Nouvelle-France (New France Route) and Chemin du Roy (King's Way).

Located north of Notre-Dame Basilica, Quebec City's **Quartier-Latin★** (Latin Quarter) is the oldest residential district in Upper Town. The narrow streets criss-crossing the quarter are remnants of the passageways that once connected these large holdings. Between 1820 and 1830, the craftsmen who initially populated the district gave way to a French-speaking bourgeoisie (read upwardly-mobile), eager to be at the center of the religious action of the day. After World War II, the bohemian lifestyle grew in Old Quebec at the same time as the Laval University was expanding into the district, occupying dozens of old houses. Today, these Old World mansions are mostly the enclave of students, young professionals, and artisan types.

monument in 1966. The most European of Quebec's churches, the graceful architectural design yields an impressive structure, bearing witness to a Who's Who of Quebec architects with names such as Baillif, Baillargé, Chaussegros de Léry, and Chênevert, among others. Many historical heavyweights are buried in the crypt here, like Frontenac, Laval, Vaudreuil, Callières, plus legions of bishops, merchants, and architects.

Hôtel de Ville de Québec
(Quebec City Hall)

2 Rue des Jardins.

A majestic structure built in 1922, this classic, late-Victorian architectural gem occupies a whole city block of sloping land formerly belonging to the Jesuits. This powerful building reflects architect Tanguay's eclectic opulence in a blend of Second Empire and French Château styles. It is also a cherished part of the UNESCO-designated

Quebec Seminary★★
Séminaire de Québec

1 Rue des Remparts. 418-692-3981. www.seminairedequebec.org.

Quebec City's Laval University began right here in 1663 as a training school for priests. In the complex around a courtyard is the **Museum of French America [M²]** *(Musée de l'Amérique Française; see map p 31),* the **oldest museum in Canada**, where historical documents, paintings, and precious religious articles of this priceless facility may be found. Inside, you'll

Quebec Seminary

© Mar Hermann Giguère PH

learn about the French-speaking communities of North America, such as Acadia, Louisiana, Saint-Boniface, and even places in New England and the Canadian West, which owe their origins to New France.

Musée de l'Amérique Française★ (Museum of French America) (M⁵)

Main entrance at 2 Côte de la Fabrique (Welcome Pavilion). Open late-Jun–Labor Day, daily 9.30am–5pm; rest of the year, Tue–Sun 10am–5pm. Closed Dec 25. $8. 418-692-2843; 1-866-710-8031. www.mcq.org.

Operated since 1995 as part of the Museum of Civilization, the collections of the Museum of French America encompass objects and works of art reflecting France's rich historic, cultural, and social heritage in North America. An extensive historical archive features

some 195,000 rare books and journals; European paintings from the 15C–19C; Canadian paintings from the 18C–20C; gold and silver religious artifacts; extensive collections of textiles, furniture, scientific instruments, stamps, coins, birds, and insects. They even have botanical, zoological, and geological specimens.

The collections are housed in three buildings, of which **Welcome Pavilion** serves as the museum's reception and information center, as well as a temporary exhibition space. The second building occupies the seminary's former outer chapel.

The building (c.1890) features an interior modeled after the 19C Trinity Church in Paris. The Quebec version, made of galvanized steel painted in trompe-l'oeil, provides better protection against fire.

In addition to beautiful pieces of silverware by Ranvoyzé, Loir, Amiot, and others, the chapel contains one of the most important collections of **relics**★ outside St. Peter's in Rome. Some of these, like the silver chalice commissioned in 1673 from France by Monsigneur de Laval himself, are still in use by local priests. The third structure is the **Jérôme Demers Pavilion**. Beat author Jack Kerouac, boasting francophone heritage, would love the permanent exhibition here called *On the Road: The Francophone Odyssey*, as it explores the evolution of geographical movement by the French throughout the continent. It presents the seven major francophone communities on the continent: Quebec, Acadia, Louisiana, French Ontario, Métis, and French-American communities in the West and in New England. The second exhibit incorporates highlights of the seminary's impressive collections to underscore the institution's religious, cultural, and educational mission. Temporary thematic exhibits here invite discovery of Quebec via its provincial arts, crafts, folklore, and history.

⊘ *Leave the museum by Rue de l'Université and turn right on Rue Sainte-Famille. Take Rue Couillard on the left.*

Charming **Rue Couillard** received its name in the 18C, in honor of the sailor Guillaume Couillard (1591–1663), son-in-law and heir to the lands of Louis Hébert. Its sinuous path leads past the former Hospice de la Miséricorde (*no. 14*), built between 1878 and 1880 for the Sisters of the Good Shepherd.

Musée Bon-Pasteur (Good Shepherd Museum)

14 Rue Couillard, between Rue Ferland and Rue Saint-Flavien. Open year-round, Tue–Sun 1pm–5pm. $3. 418-694-0243. www.museebonpasteur.com.

This remarkable Gothic Revival structure, with its brick walls pierced by arched windows, was once the infamous Hôpital de la Miséricorde (Hospital of Mercy). It also housed the Mercy Hospice, operated by the Sœurs du Bon-Pasteur (Sisters of the Good Shepherd) as a refuge and halfway house for marginalized women of the day. Today, the structure has been renovated as a museum tracing the history of the Good Shepherd community, a lay order founded in 1850 by Marie-du-Sacré-Cœur (aka Marie Fitzbach). Artifacts, sculptures, furnishings, musical instruments, and articles of daily life illustrate the caring and teaching vocations of the sisters, life in the community, and the activities of the order today.

Musée Bon-Pasteur

© Perry Mastrovito/Age Fotostock

▷ *Turn right on Rue Collins and continue to Rue Charlevoix.*

Monastère de l'Hôtel-Dieu de Québec
(Augustine Monastery)

32 Rue Charlevoix.

These founding sisters of the first hospital in North America north of Mexico *(onsite)* took up residence in Sillery before moving to Quebec proper. In 1644, upon completion of their monastery, the nuns moved to this site in the old city primarily to aid the native population. The first hospital erected by the nuns was made of wood and contained one of the few interior staircases anywhere.

In 1695, François de la Joüe enlarged the structure by annexing a stone building; the two structures now form part of the convent and can be clearly seen from the garden. The hospital underwent several expansions during the 19C and 20C, reaching its current capacity in 1960.

Musée des Augustines de l'Hôtel-Dieu de Québec★
(Augustine Museum)

32 Rue Charlevoix. Open year-round, Tue–Sat 9.30am–noon, 1.30pm–5pm, Sun 1.30pm–5pm. Closed major holidays. 418-692-2492. www.museocapitale.qc.ca.

Initially opened in 1958 to celebrate the 350th Anniversary of the founding of Quebec, the museum presents a collection of objects and artworks tracing the Augustinian nuns' humanitarian history and heritage in New France. It includes one of the foremost collections of medical instruments; surgical, ENT, and dental tools. The nuns were also female apothecaries, as witnessed by the presence of pill boxes, scalpels, mortars and pestles, and various accessories for practicing anesthesiology and pharmacology.

Church★

Same hours as museum.

To counteract the proliferation of non-Catholic community chapels that appeared in Quebec City with the influx of Protestant-Irish immigrants in the early 19C, the Church of Quebec encouraged the nuns to erect a large Catholic church. Designed by Pierre Émond in 1800, under the supervision of Father Jean-Louis Desjardins, the structure features polygonal chapels and an apse, connected to the convent.

The Neoclassical facade (1835) boasts a beautifully sculpted Ionic portal created by Thomas Baillargé. The small belfry was placed over the facade in 1931.

The sculpted, gilded wood **interior décor** was finished in 1832, and is highlighted by the **high-altar tabernacle**, a small-scale model of St. Peter's in Rome; the retable, in the shape of a triumphal arch; and the basket-handle wooden vault. The painting above the altar, *The Descent from the Cross*, executed by Antoine Plamondon in 1840, was inspired by Rubens' famous masterpiece, which now hangs in Antwerp Cathedral in Belgium. The church features a collection of paintings confiscated from churches in Paris during the Revolution and sent to Quebec in 1817.

FORTIFICATIONS★★

The defenses of Quebec City were not solely built by the French. The British added Martello towers to the works of French military engineers, and completed the Citadel between 1820 and 1832. Once the British garrison moved on in 1871, Lord Dufferin, the Governor-General, decided on major renovations and restoration to beautify the city, and visitors are in his debt to this day.

Royal 22e Régiment Museum La Citadelle National Historic Site★★

South of the Upper Town, from inside the St-Louis Gate. Visit by guided tour only, Apr 10am–4pm, May–Sep 9am–5pm, Oct 10am–3pm. Nov–Mar daily tour at 1.30pm. $10. 418-694-2815. www.lacitadelle.qc.ca.

Sitting atop the most strategic military perch on the continent, Cap Diamant (Cape Diamond), La Citadelle stands watch over the gigantic Saint Lawrence River below, entry point to the Great Lakes and the North American continent beyond.
Planned by the French, construction was actually finished in 1820 by the British and remains the largest fortress in North America built by the Brits. A star-shaped layout, the site includes a system of fortified outworks protecting the landward side from attack, while cannon on solid ramparts guards the city from a seaward assault. Had the French completed this wonderful defensive work earlier, they might have been spared the embarrassment of 1759, when the English unexpectedly approached from the landward side.
La Citadelle is an active military base for the Royal 22nd Regiment—the French-speaking "Van Doos." Don't miss their 🎺 **Changing of the Guard** ceremony, in full-dress scarlet uniform, at 10am from June 24 to the first weekend of September.

Changing of the Guard, La Citadelle

©J. Beardsell

FORTIFICATIONS

Hôtel Glace Québec-Canada (New Location)

Now located more conveniently at the Quebec Zoo: *9530 Rue de la Faune, 418-623-2888, www. icehotel-canada.com. Open beginning Jan–end of Mar only. 36 rooms and theme suites.* Sleep inside a real Nordic cacoon, with ice chandeliers nearby and even an Ice Chapel. Wind chill doesn't apply when you are comfy inside this ice sculpture, snug on a bed inside an Arctic sleeping bag. They're lining up to get into the Ice Hotel, with visitors making reservations a year ahead.

©D. Reeve/Michelin

Come visit and take the guided tour (*$17.50*) of the 3,250-sq m (35,000-sq ft) ice creation. Overnight packages include breakfast, drinks, dinner, Welcome kit, and a room at the Sheraton Four Points.

Governors' Walk★★
Promenade des Gouverneurs

⊳ *Leave the Citadel by the Durnford Gate, take the path to the left and continue toward the St. Lawrence River.*

Continue from La Citadelle to **Dufferin Terrace★★★** *(Terrasse Dufferin)*, a wooden platform and public park conceived by Governor-General Dufferin to afford magnificent **views★★** of the river. Onward, just before the Château Frontenac in Jardin des Gouverneurs park, the **Wolfe-Montcalm Monument [1]** *(see map p 31)* commemorates the British and French commanders of 1759, who both died in the Battle of the Plains of Abraham. The Dufferin Terrace is also the place to be for winter carnival's thrilling quarter-mile **Toboggan Run**.

Artillery Park National Historic Site★
Lieu Historique National du Canada du Parc-de-l'Artillerie

2 Rue d'Auteuil. Open daily Apr–Sep 10am–6pm, Sep–Oct 10am–5pm. $4. 418-648-4205. www.pc.gc.ca/artillery.

Continuing along the walls to face the modern city, you'll come to the site of a British artillery barracks and later, a Canadian arms works and arsenal. The **Old Foundry, Dauphine Redoubt**, and **Officers' Quarters** are the focal points, including a scale model of Quebec City, a look inside this remarkable four-story 1712 structure, and more.

GRANDE ALLÉE★

From the St-Louis Gate, the Grande Allée leads into the new city in appropriately grand fashion. Boutiques, restaurants, and nightclubs line the sidewalks, while trees and 19C mansions and town houses give it the air of a small-scale European boulevard. Begin the walking tour at the Parliament Building. *(5km/3mi.)*

Parliament Building★★
Hôtel du Parlement

Visit via Entrance #3, Grand Allée & Honoré-Mercier Ave. Visit by guided tour only, 1st Tuesday Sep–Jun 23, Mon–Fri 9am–4.30pm, Jun 24– Labor Day, Mon–Fri 9.00–4.30pm, Sat/Sun 10.00–4.30pm. 418-643- 7239. www.assnat.qc.ca.

The Government of the Province of Quebec is called the National Assembly. It sits in this fine Second Empire building inaugurated in 1876. In scale and size, it's reminiscent of city halls of the era in other parts of the continent, but the decorative stonework and delicate ironwork feel like Paris.

Quebec Museum of Fine Arts ★★
(Musée National des Beaux-Arts du Québec)

Parc de Champs-de-Bataille, via Grand-Allée to Avenue Wolfe- Montcalm. Open Jun–early Sept, daily 10am–6pm (Wed 9pm); rest of the year, Tue–Sun 10am–5pm (Wed 9pm). Closed Dec 25. $15. 418-644- 6450. www.mnba.qc.ca.

Situated on the site of the Parc des Champs-de-Bataille (Battlefields Park), this remarkable museum complex (a former prison) provides a overview of Quebec art from the 18C to the present. Quebec's art icons, Jean-Paul Riopelle and Jean-Paul Lemieux are showcased.

Exhibits draw from a collection of over 23,000 works of art, including those of the former Brousseau Museum of Inuit Art (**M**[1]) and are organized in three buildings.

National Battlefields Park★
Parc des Champs-de-Bataille

834 Ave. Wilfred-Laurier. Discovery Pavilion open July 24–Labor Day 8.30am–5.30pm; rest of year Mon–Fri 8.30am–5pm, Sat 9am–5pm, Sun 10am–5pm. $5. 418-648-6157. www.ccbn-nbc.gc.ca.

Here, on the Plains of Abraham in 1759, British troops under General Wolfe scaled the cliffs undetected, and in less than 15 minutes put an end to the French Empire in North America. Skirmishes raged for several years, but this is where the fate of the Continent was decided. Three Martello towers remain from the days of the British garrison, erected as a defense against the Americans, who had occupied Quebec City during the winter of 1775–76. The only access was via a ladder, pulled up once you entered. The city's UNESCO status is in large part owed to these fortifications. On the grounds of the park is the **Quebec Museum of Fine Arts★★** *(Musée National des Beaux-Arts du Québec)* housing significant Quebec art from the last two centuries.

EXCURSIONS

Passion for life is legend in "La Belle Province" and visible in what the locals call the "regions." Just watch the crowds exiting either city on weekends, and you'll understand how residents love to savor their vast province. Travelers who follow will discover lush geography, quaint villages with inns and eateries, and friendly people near either city.

THE EASTERN TOWNSHIPS★★

Cantons de l'Est or l'Estrie

▷ *Take Autoroute 10 (via Champlain Bridge) to the Eastern Townships Autoroute (#10) directly east from Montreal.*

Bounded by the St. Lawrence and Richelieu Rivers, and the US states of Vermont, Maine, and New Hampshire, the proximity of the Appalachians gives the Townships their meadows, forests, and mountain ridges such as Sutton, Bromont, and Orford. British loyalists who fled the former American colonies after the Treaty gave the towns their character, as lost corners of New England. Remnants of these independent farmers and tradesmen who settled here can still be seen in their old clapboard and brick farmhouses and red barns—distinct from the stone farmsteads of the St. Lawrence Valley.

Villages here reflect this 19C ambiance in communities filled with artists, antique merchants, and literary types. The entrepreneurial spirit is alive and well with brew pubs, bookstores, and B&Bs heralding their independence.

Granby Zoo★
Jardin Zoologique de Granby

1050, Boulevard David-Bouchard (Hwy. #139), Granby, ▷ 83km/52mi east of Montreal via Autoroute 10 to Exit 68, north on Hwy. 139. Open late May–mid-June 10am–5pm, mid-June–late-Aug 10am–7pm; zoo open daily through Labour Day & weekends to early Oct 10am–5pm. $34 adults, $22 children aged 3–12, children under 2 free. 450-372-9113 or 877-472-6299. www.zoogranby.ca.

Brilliant tropical parrots in the Great North? Why not! Not to mention Japanese monkeys, Siberian tigers, a snow leopard, and kangaroos and wallabees. This is an up-close zoo, and aquarium, too, where visitors can pass their hands through fur and feathers, pet nurse sharks and manta rays, and stare their animal friends straight in the eyes. Check out the new **South Pacific Pavilion** and the **Night Safari**.

Lake Brome★
Lac-Brome

▷ *110km/68mi east of Montreal via Autoroute 10 east to Exit 90, then south on Hwy. 243.*

Browse antique shops, art galleries, and **Knowlton**, where you'll also find a bastion of English language theater performances presented at the **Brome Lake Theatre**, or live music at the **Haskell Opera House** down the road in Stanstead. For more country fun, try the **Brome Agricultural Fair** in early September. And for a real taste of the area, try ordering Brome Duck served at any fine table in Quebec, and always on the menu at local restaurants.

Brome County Museum★ *130 Rue Lakeside, Knowlton. 450-243-6782. Open mid-May–mid-Sep daily 11am–4.30pm. $5. www.townshipsheritage.com.* This collection of heritage buildings includes the original schoolhouse, fire house (converted to a general store), and brick courthouse.

Parc National du Mont-Orford★

◯ *128km/80mi east of Montreal via Autoroute 10 to Exit 115, then Hwy. 141 north. Skiing, boating, and golf. Admission $5.50 daily, $5 parking, additional costs for activities, rentals, etc. 819-843-6548 or 866-673-6731; www.orford.com. Park: 819-843-9855; www.sepaq.com.*

An island of wilderness in a long-settled rural area, Mount Orford

(850m/2,788ft) is best known for its family-oriented **downhill skiing**, with a vertical drop of 540m/1,771ft, and 54 trails. Every sort of skiing is available, from daredevil to beginner, and every kind of lift, from gondola to quadruple chairs to old-fashioned T-bar and rope tow.

Mount Orford Golf Club is easily one of the most picturesque in the province, *(inexpensive at $35 for 18 holes).* Swimming, cycling, and climbing round off the top outdoor summer activities, with the entire area ablaze with color in the fall. Great live concerts Jul through Aug at the **Centre d'Arts Orford** *(Orford Arts Centre; 800-567-6155; www.arts-orford.org).*

St-Benoît-du-Lac Abbey★
Abbaye de St-Benôit-du-Lac

◯ *20km/12mi west of Magog via Route 112; turn south after 5km/3mi and continue 2km/1.24mi past Austin. Open daily 9am–4.30pm. 819-843-4080. www.st-benoit-du-lac.com. Men's Guesthouse, 819-843-2340. $50 per night.*

©Stéphane Lemire / Tourisme Canton-de-l'Est

St-Benoît-du-Lac-Abbey

The Benedictine abbey and its bell tower rise from Lake Memphremagog on a knoll as if they've always been there. Actually, the abbey was founded in 1924; most of the buildings went up in the 1930s according to the plans of renowned monk-architect Dom Paul Bellot, who is buried here. The church was consecrated in 1994. The monks follow lives of prayer and contemplation, but also manual work. They run cheese and cider factories and an orchard, and accept both men and women for retreats *(reserve by telephone only)*. Day visitors are welcome to browse the small shop and buy cheese until 10.45am, to hear the 11am Mass complete with Gregorian chants, and to hear vespers at 5pm *(except on Thursday)*. At other times, you can appreciate the abbey from the waters of Lake Memphremagog, and purchase the excellent L'Ermite and Mont-Saint-Benoît cheeses in shops nearby.

Sutton★

◯ *123km/77mi east of Montreal via Autoroute 10 to Exit 68, then south on Hwy. 139.*

First Nations lived here for 3,000 years before the Americans settled in 1795. Boutiques and galleries open all year; golfers are active, too. Ask about the **Wine Trail**. Hiking covers 270km/168 mi of bliss. **Mount Sutton** *450-538-2545, www.montsutton.com* is one of the premier ski areas in the Townships, boasting 53 trails descending from a long ridge, including significant expanses of Quebec's famous glade skiing, a 968m/3,194ft summit, nine chairlifts, and a 455m/1,500ft vertical drop over 70ha/175 acres.

Lake Memphremagog

◯ *124km/78mi east of Montreal via Autoroute 10 east to Exit 115 for Magog.*

This fresh water glacial lake stretches 50km/31mi between ridges of mountains and hills from Magog down to Newport, Vermont. Steamers connect with stage coaches to provide transport to the south. Old inns survive to cater to today's travelers, whether they're in search of traditional surroundings, or looking for Memphry *(Memphré)*, the monster who reputedly lurks beneath the waves. Winds are reliable, making Memphremagog the preferred lake in Quebec for sailing and windsurfing.

Lake Cruises★

Le Grande Cru (new boat) departs Macpherson Pier in Magog. 819-843-7000. www.escapadesmemphremagog.com. $30 (4pm–6pm), $65 (brunch), or $85 (gourmet dinner); packages with accommodation from $100. Operates mid-Jun 1–mid-Oct 11am–7pm (call to reserve). The best way to reach the hidden coves of **Lake Mvemphremagog** and view its historic houses, lakeside estates, and the mountains to the west and south, is to board one of the cruise boats that make daily trips in summer. Visitors will maximize on both their ability to view the surrounding mountains and sights, plus the benefit of being able to explore all the nooks and crannies of this glacier lake in a relatively small craft *(170 passengers)*. The evening cruise is the best value.

MUST SEE

Mont-Tremblant

©Richard Nowitz/Apa Publications

Almost as pleasing as sailing or motorboating is exploring the winding roads above the lake by car, on foot, or bicycle, catching the views to the Green Mountains of Vermont, and nearby Mount Orford and Owl's Head. The town of **Magog★** *(take Autoroute 10 to Hwy. 112)*, at the northern end of the lake, and **Bleu Lavande** to the East, an idyllic lavender field haven for mind, body, and spirit.

THE LAURENTIANS★★

Les Laurentides

🔗 *60km/37mi north of Montreal via Route 15. www.laurentians.com.*

Over 22,000 sq km/13,670 sq mi features the oldest mountains in the world. Unbroken expanses of forested mountain lead to crystal-clear lakes, superb skiing, hiking, watersports, and fishing, plus year-round resorts. Chefs settle here and visitors benefit at tables set for kings. You can even take AMT regional trains from downtown Montreal to Saint-Jerome *(www. amt.qc.ca)*, rent bikes, or bring your own, and explore over 200km/120mi of the **Le P'tit Train**

du Nord, the longest linear park in Canada, created on the old skier's train path through the mountains. Eateries, inns, galleries, spas, and villages wind all the way to **Mont-Laurier**. Walking, riding, or skiing this trail through the mountains is the perfect way to savor local character, embrace the land, and have fun.

Mont-Tremblant Park★
Parc du Mont-Tremblant

🔗 *136km/84mi north via Autoroute 15 & Hwy. 117 to St-Faustin, then right on Rue Principale, then Chemin du Lac-Supérieur. Day pass $10. Rentals & camping extra. 819-688-2289. www.sepaq.com.*

Mont-Tremblant marks the beginning of the largest park in the province, filled with forests, lakes, rivers, and hills. Deer, moose, black bears,z and wolves call the park home, along with the endangered bald eagle. In winter, visitors may drive from Tremblant Village and follow a road that winds along the twisting Rivière du Diable (Devil's River) to the exciting **Chûtes Croches** (falls). Summer allows a circular trip along the river past

Mont-Tremblant: Mountain, Village, Resort

At 875m/2,871ft, Tremblant is the tallest peak in the Laurentians. The chairlift to the top *(one of 14)* operates year-round, except during high winds, and **views** are breathtaking. The 95 marked ski trails ranging from easy to double black diamond highlight this Intrawest resort location. The inns, shops, and steep-roofed houses of the lakeside village retain the charm of years gone by, with many artisan boutiques found nowhere else. Accessible via the nearby airport, the lake stretches fjord-like 12km/7.5mi up the valley. Just steps from the lifts, Station Mont-Tremblant resort *(514-876-7273 or 866-356-2233. www.tremblant.ca)*, is a state-of-the-art walking village with 1,900 rooms in hotels and condos, along with shops, restaurants, and resort services. In warmer months, golf and watersports are the main activities, with the lake and rivers to suit, and numerous challenging golf courses nearby.

the **Devil's Falls★** and **Muskrat Falls★**, and back to continue to St-Donat, or onward toward Sainte-Agathe. Park adventures include cross-country skiing and snowshoeing in winter, and hiking, climbing, parasailing, cycling, and fishing in summer. You can rent canoes and kayaks in the park, or at Lac Supérieur, just east of Mont-Tremblant village, or even rent a log chalet at **Côté-Nord Tremblant** (www.cotenordtremblant.com) and dine lakeside at their **Caribou Lodge**.

Sainte-Adèle★

The Laurentian Autoroute *(Autoroute 15)* twists up into the Laurentians, and the older road *(Hwy. 117)* winds with even more turns on the way north, past mountains speckled with ski resorts, condos, and eateries. Sainte-Adèle *(Exit 67)*, set around a small lake, offers nearby slopes to suit differing tastes.

Côtes 40–80 *(Hill 40–80)* is an unpretentious set of moderate and intermediate runs, embellished with new equipment and popular ski boarding zones too. At the higher end is **Le Chantecler** *(888-*

916-1616)* encompassing several peaks and a ski-in, ski-out hotel.

Saint-Sauveur-des Monts★

⊙ *60km/37mi northwest of Montreal via Autoroute 15 north to Exit 60.*

Saint-Sauveur marks the major ski area closest to Montreal. **Mont St-Sauveur** and **Mont-Avila** *(450-227-4671 or 514-871-0101; www.montsaintsauveur.com)*, just off Autoroute 15 at kilometre 60 are jointly operated, with interconnecting trails. St-Sauveur has a maximum 230m/700ft drop, 38 trails, and extremely fast chairlifts that pack skiers onto the slopes. Mont-Avila has a **tube slide** in addition to ski trails. Once the snow's gone, water slides and pools keep visitors coming. The huge wooden Mont St-Sauveur ski lodge was considered a landmark building when it opened in 1977. For a quick escape, drive 40 minutes up to Saint-Sauveur on a late winter's afternoon and buy a reduced-rate ticket for **night skiing**. Ski traffic is lighter than during the day and the 38 trails are well-lit for

MUST SEE

an adventure that can be enjoyed in relatively few resorts. You'll be back in Montreal by bedtime.

Val-David

◗ *80km/48mi north of Montreal via Autoroute 15 to Exit 76.*

One of the most idyllic village settings in the mountains offers visitors the combination of atmosphere, services, and attractions in one place. The Rivière du Nord ambles through a town stocked with potters, painters, blacksmiths, and more.

WEST ISLAND AND BEYOND★★

◗ *West of downtown Montreal. Métro Lionel-Groulx, then bus 211 (221 rush hour) to Pointe-Claire or Sainte-Anne, or train from Windsor Station.*

It's called *L'Ouest de l'Île* in French, or more usually *Le West-Island*, in recognition of the English-speaking character of this part of Montreal. Bedroom suburbs take up much of the terrain, but a number of formerly independent towns preserve their heritage architecture. **Lachine** is the terminus of the Lachine Canal, site of the **Fur Trade Museum** *(see Museums)*. You can visit most of these sites in an easy half-day excursion by municipal bus.

Pointe-Claire Village★

◗ *22km/14mi west of Montreal via Route 20 to Exit 50, left on Boul. St-Jean to Lac St. Louis, village right.*

Antique shops, tearooms, a pub, florist, yacht club, ice-cream shop and others line the streets of this

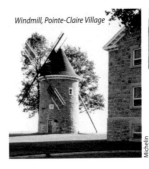
Windmill, Pointe-Claire Village

Michelin

quiet village. They've survived the winds of change that have sent shoppers and businesses to the malls in other suburbs, and flourished among clients who appreciate smaller and slower. Get off the bus or park your car where Avenue Cartier meets Lakeshore Road *(Bord-du-Lac)*, and take time to stroll Pointe-Claire Village and browse the curio shops.

The old **windmill** on the point survives from 1709, when its solid wall provided refuge during attacks. The **Couvent Notre-Dame-de-Vieux-Moulin** convent dates from 1867, the church from 1882. Stroll eastward along Lakeshore Road to appreciate the superb river **views** and the substantial houses that face the water. Past Boulevard St-Jean is **Stewart Hall★**, a half-scale replica of a Scottish Manor now used as a cultural center.

Sainte-Anne-de-Bellevue★

◗ *34km/21mi west of Montreal via Autoroute 20 to Exit 39.*

A mixed English- and French-speaking village, in summer Sainte-Anne fills up when visitors seek its waterside cafes and

Fraternité-sur-Lac/Côté Nord Tremblant
North Side of Mont-Tremblant

Two sister developments overlook Lac Superior 90min from Montreal and allow visitors to explore a different character to mountain and lake.

Six minutes from Northside slopes, an entire new village boasts a more relaxed ambiance without lacking creature comforts. Rent one of 50 log chalets from Côté Nord Tremblant *(888-268-3667)* complete with 2–5 bedrooms, fireplace, full kitchen, A/C, TV, phone, and Wi-Fi, or the village creation of Fraternité-sur-Lac. Both projects have access to pool, tennis, kayaks, and skiing *(www.fraternitesurlac.com)*.

offbeat shops. An old set of locks still provides safe passage from the Ottawa River into the St. Lawrence.

Sainte-Anne Church (1853) occupies the site of the 1703 chapel, where fur traders prayed before undertaking perilous trips to the West. The **Simon Fraser/ Tom Moore House** *(153 Rue Ste-Anne)* was acquired by **The Canadian Heritage Foundation**. It has a tearoom run by the V.O.N. Auxiliary, and a museum run by the Historical Society of Bout de l'Isle. Characterized by stone foundations, **Hudson Bay House** *(9 Rue Ste-Anne)* served variously as a trading post, a Mounties' barracks and a hotel. **Sainte-Anne-de-Bellevue Canal National Historic Site** – Once part of a busy inland shipping route to Ottawa and the Great Lakes, now mostly sees pleasure boats and occasionally an organized cruise *(bit.ly/IKPg77; 514-457-5546)*.
Sainte Anne Surroundings – Located on Rue Ste-Anne, McGill University's agricultural school occupies the **Macdonald Campus**. You can visit the extensive collection of the **Lyman Entomological Museum** *(open Mon–Fri 9am–5pm; 514-398-7914)*.

Morgan Arboretum is the university's forest reserve, home to over 200 bird species. It's a favored cross-country ski area in winter *(150 Chemin des Pins, off Chemin Sainte-Marie; open daily 9am–4pm, grounds open until sunset; $5 to walk, $6 to ski; 514-398-7811; www.morgan arboretum.org)*.

Île Perrot

◷ *45km/28mi west of Montreal via Autoroute 20.*

Just off the western end of Montreal, this island is still partially rural, and retains vestiges of the French regime.

Church of St. Jeanne of Chantal★
(Église Sainte-Jeanne-de Chantal)
Rue de l'Église, Village-sur-le-Lac (south sector of island). Open for tours by appointment only, Jul–Aug Mon–Fri 10am–5pm, weekends 9am–5pm. 514-453-2125. www.paroissesjc.org.
This late-18C stone church recalls rural life before Île Perrot was a suburb of Montreal. Early-19C sculptures by Joseph Turcaut and Louis-Xavier Leprohon remain inside.

MUST SEE

**Pointe-du-Moulin
Historic Park★**
*(Parc historique Pointe-du-Moulin)
2500 Boul. Don-Quichotte. Open
mid-May–Oct 9.30am–5pm, until
9pm in summer. $5. 514-453-5936.
www.pointedumoulin.com.*
A restored mill is in working
operation. Exhibits in the miller's
house illustrate the rural way
of life in New France, including
old-fashioned breadmaking. **Views**
stretch to the distant Adirondack
mountains in New York State.

Vaudreuil-Dorion

◐ *50km/31mi west of Montreal
via Autoroute 20.*

First municipality on the mainland
retains grand historic houses, but
reflects the developer's touch too,
as former farmland turns to condos
and malls. Don't miss **Château
Vaudreuil** *(800-363-7896)* for
idyllic setting lakeside.

Trestler House★
(Maison Trestler)

◐ *85 Chemin de la Commune,
Dorion. Follow Rue St-Henri
north from Autoroute 20, then
Rue Trestler east. 450-455-6920.
www.trestler.qc.ca. Open Mon–Fri
10am–noon & 1pm–4pm, Sunday
1pm–4pm. Bilingual tours. $4.*
Regular cultural events highlight
this impressive waterside mansion
erected by a mercenary who
came out on the losing side in the
American Revolution.
Johan-Josef Trestler, like many of
his comrades in arms, integrated
into the French-Canadian
community. He established a
combination fur trading outpost/
general store/mansion/fortress.
Some rooms still sport 18C and 19C

furnishings, while the **view** of Two
Mountains is spectacular along Lac
Saint-Louis.

LANAUDIÈRE

Generations of Montrealers have
gone northeast to Lanaudière to
fish, hunt, and listen to beautiful
music in quintessentially French-
Canadian villages, where the forests
of the Canadian Shield begin.

Joliette★

◐ *75km/46mi from Montreal by
Autoroute 40 & Autoroute 31.*

Musicians of world renown perform
at the **Festival International de
Lanaudière** *(early Jul through
early Aug)* in an amphitheater in
the woods, and in the churches of
Quebec's summer cultural capital
(www.lanaudiere.org).
Joliette Art Museum *(Musée d'Art
de Joliette) 145 Rue Pére- Wilfrid-
Corbeil. 450-756-0311. Open Jun–
Aug Tue–Sun noon–5pm. $10.
www.musee.joliette.org.* This
premier Quebec museum displays
early works reflecting a vision of
God adapted to a remote colony, as
well as paintings by modern artists.
Cathedral – *2 Rue St-Charles
Borromée Nord. Open year-
round Tue–Fri 11.30am–3.30pm;
weekends 2pm–5pm.* A domed
Romanesque structure, the
cathedral showcases vaults and
columns worthy of Europe cities,
as well as polished wood floors
characteristic of Quebec's artisan
legacy. From Joliette, wind along
Highway 131.
The fabled spring thaw brings
out the best of the **Seven Falls of
Saint-Zénon★**, 20km/12mi past
Sainte-Émélie-de-l'Énergie *(450-
884-0484; www.haute-matawinie.*

St-Lambert and the Seaway

Opposite Parc Jean-Drapeau. Métro Longueuil, then bus 1 to Écluse (Lock); or Autoroute 20 service road to the sign for Écluse. Head out to St. Lambert for an up-close view of operations on the St. Lawrence Seaway, the set of embankments, canals, and 2 major **locks★** *(St-Lambert/St.Catherine)* allowing ocean ships to sail past Montreal and onward to the Great Lakes. Just beyond the locks, you can watch the two sections of the **Victoria Bridge★** rise and fall to allow Seaway and motorized traffic to move continuously. You won't see an equivalent feat of engineering unless you go all the way to Panama.

com; open mid-May–Nov daily
9.30am–6pm; |$5). Be sure to see
Bridal Veil Falls (*Voile de la mariée*)
in May; once the 60m/197ft falls
dry up in June, it's all the better
for hiking.

THE SOUTH SHORE★

Rive-Sud/Monterégie
Reaching away from Montreal
across the Jacques-Cartier,
Champlain, and Victoria bridges,
through suburbs and into
flat, fertile farmland, the Saint
Lawrence River Valley exposes the
Monteregian Hills; **Mont-Saint-
Gregoire**, **Mont Saint-Bruno**,
and others, while on a clear day

the **Appalachian Mountains**
tempt in the form of Vermont's
Green Mountains chain, and
New York's **White Mountains**.
These formations provide great
opportunities for sport and
pleasure, all within a short drive
of the city limits.

Fort Chambly National Historic Site★★
Lieu Historique National du Canada du Fort-Chambly

◐ *30km/19mi south of Montreal via Autoroute 10 east, then north on Hwy. 133. 2 Rue de Richelieu, Chambly. Open 10am–5pm, Apr–mid-Oct. 450-658-1585. www.pc.gc.ca. $5.*

Fort Chambly National Historic Site

©Parks Canada / A.Choquette

Located on the Richelieu River at the Chambly white-water falls, this imposing stone fort is the only fortification remaining from the **French Regime**. Restored by Parks Canada, and protected by the famous ramparts, you may view multimedia exihibitions showcasing artifacts and recreating the life of the garrison during the regime. Enjoy summertime military exercises, period dress, and fun activities.

its bastions. Ride the **ferry** to visit the fort and appreciate its strategic setting guarding the river. **Barracks**, **guardhouse**, **prison**, and **officers' quarters** are ordered and symmetrical, mirroring inflexible British field tactics and formations.

Îles-de-Boucherville National Park
Parc National des Îles-de-Boucherville

◗ *15km/9m northeast of Montreal via Hwy. 138 to Autoroute 25 to Parc de l'Île-Charron.* **Métro Honoré-Beaugrand, green line, then bus 185 or Métro Assomption to bus 22. 450-928-5088. www.sepaq.com.**

An unexpected wilderness lies on the uninhabited Isles of Boucherville, which are crossed by canals, covered by marshland, traversed by cycling and foot trails, and connected by footbridges. For a delightful experience, rent a rowboat, canoe or kayak, and paddle through the islands. Golf inside the park at the Graham Cooke-designed Golf des Iles *(www.golfdesiles.com).*

> **Getting to the Islands**
> **River shuttles** run to Île Charron/Îles-de-Boucherville Park from Promenade Bellerive in Bellerive Park *(late-Jun–early-Sept; $5).* For information, call Societé de l'Animation de la Promenade Bellerive *514-493-1967.*

Fort Lennox National Historic Site★
Lieu Historique National du Canada du Fort-Lennox

◗ *60km/38mi south of Montreal. Take Autoroute 10 east to Autoroute 35, then south to St-Jean-sur-Richelieu; then Rte. 233 south to St-Paul-de-l' Île aux Noix.* **Open mid-May–mid-Oct Mon–Fri 10am–5pm. $8, including parking, taxes and return ferry ride. 450-291-5700. www.pc.gc.ca.**

Île aux Noix (Walnut Island) is the site of this 19C star-shaped British defensive work, state-of-the-art for its day and surrounded by a moat. Fort Lennox was completed in 1829, just in time for an easing of tension with the Americans, and no angry shot was ever fired from

Kahnawake

◗ *12km/7mi south of Montreal via Hwy. 138 and the Mercier Bridge.* **Buses leave from Angrignon Métro station. www.kahnawake.com.**

Lying opposite the western end of Montreal, each July the Mohawk community of Kahnawake ("above the rapids") celebrates its heritage at the **Echoes of a Proud Nation Pow-Wow**, which features traditional Iroquois smoke dancers, singing, drumming, etc.

EXCURSIONS

Fort Blunder

Farther upriver at Rouses Point you'll find **Fort Montgomery** (or Fort Blunder as it's known), on the shores of Lake Champlain. The US outpost was abandoned when troops discovered it was on the Canadian side of the border.

QUEBEC CITY AREA

Sillery and Sainte-Foy

❍ *Drive west from Old Town along Avenue Grande-Allée.*

Located on the banks of the St. Lawrence barely 1km/0.6mi from Quebec, the community of Sillery was named after a French nobleman. This quaint neighborhood was founded in 1637 by Jesuits trying to evangelize Amerindians. Mostly what the locals got from the French was odd diseases and bad habits. After the Conquest, Jesuits made money renting to wealthy merchants, and with the ever-expanding lumber and shipbuilding industries, an economic surge happened here in the mid-19C.

Sillery's coves and bays were ideal for European ships unloading, squaring off, warehousing, and exporting goods. Sprawling mansions appeared during this prosperous era, and were occupied by some of the many religious côteries. Sillery evolved as one of the residential suburbs-of-choice for Quebec City government types. Today, a weave of Old World charm and hyperactive mall shops find a natural equilibrium.

Université Laval (Laval University)

❍ *West from the city along Avenue Grand-Allée, which becomes Avenue Laurier, continue to just before Hwy. 740 (university on your right). Métrobus 800 & 801. 418-656-7266. www.ulaval.ca.*

This is the first French-language Catholic university in North America. The original school was part of the Séminaire de Québec, founded by namesake Monseignor François de Laval way back in 1633. This current site was established in 1852, with the university itself constructing the new campus *(cité universitaire)* in this western suburb of Quebec City in 1949.

The north–south axis provides a singular view of the Laurentian Mountains, while the east–west focuses on the Grand Seminary and the **Faculty of Medicine**. There are 400 programs in 17 faculties, with over 200 research centers, and affiliations with 87 other international schools. Laval also features a **Museum of Geology** and the Roger-Van den Hende Gardens, an internationally heralded botanical collection.

Cartier-Brébeuf National Historic Site of Canada★

❍ *From Old Quebec take Rue de la Couronne to Hwy. 175 north (73 North). Exit at Rue de l'Espinay and follow signs. Open mid- May–Labor Day, daily 10am–5pm; rest of Sept, Wed–Sun 11am–4pm; rest of year by reservation. $3.90. 418-648-4038. www.pc.gc.ca/brebeuf*

Located on the northern shore of the Saint-Charles River, this site is

Cartier-Brébeuf National Historic Site of Canada

©Parks Canada

a two-for-one commemorating the first shocking winter spent in New France, near the settlement of Stadacona by Cartier in 1536, and the subsequent establishment of the first Jesuit mission by Jean de Brébeuf in 1625. The Interpretation Centre boasts museum-quality scale models, recalling Cartier's second voyage to New France and his meetings with Iroquois, plus rare nautical instruments and maps.

Charlesbourg

⊘ *From Quebec City drive north on Hwy. 175 (aka 73) and Exit 150, right on Boulevard Louis-XiV.*

Locals know this community just north of Quebec City for the wealth of cross-country skiing trails starting here, and the amazing historical preservation of the curious original town planning.

Wendake

⊘ *Drive Hwy.175 north from the city (or Free shuttle from Old Town), to 973, then 73, and follow to Exit 150. Go west along Boul. Louis-XiV,*

which becomes Boul. Bastien. Tourism Wendake is at 100 Boul. Bastien. Open Mon–Fri 8.30am–4.30pm, Sat/Sun 9am–5pm in summer. 418-847-1835. www.hotelpremiersnations.ca.

Once part of a mammoth First Nation extending across Quebec, Ontario, and Michigan, when the Europeans came, disease and intertribal wars scattered tribes across the continent. The Hurons sought protection from the French in the mid-17C. In 1668, they emigrated to Sainte-Foy, on the present site of Laval U, then to Wendake in 1697. Today, a stroll through the streets of their **Huron Village** (Village-des-Hurons) reveals the uniqueness of this place. Stay over at the awesome **Hotel-Musée Premieres Nations** *(418-847-2222)*, where contemporary, sustainable boutique hotel meets Amerindian museum/architecture. Dine on inventive traditional foods stylized for today onsite at **La Traite Restaurant**. Worth the 15-minute ride outside the city.

Site Traditionnel Huron-Eendat Onhoüa Chetek★
(Huron-Wendat Onhoüa Chetek Traditional Site)

575 Rue Stanislas-Kosca, Village-des-Hurons (Wendake). Visit by guided tour (45min) only, May–mid-Oct, daily 9am–5pm. At other times call. 418-842-4308. www.huron-wendat.qc.ca. $12.

This recreated traditional Amerindian village offers an introduction to the history, heritage, and customs of the Huron First Nation.

EXCURSIONS

SPORTS AND ACTIVITIES

Montreal is a magnet of entertaining options for travelers, no matter how active or relaxed your lifestyle. Winter or summer, you'll find adventure with gusto, or peace with panasse, either works in Quebec.

🐎 Calèche Ride in Old Montreal★★

Place d'Armes or Rue de la Commune, Old Montreal. Métro Place-d'Armes. $45/30min, $75/hr.

To best view the romantic streets of **Old Montreal★★★** try a horse-drawn carriage ride, straight out of the 19C. To hire one, go to either Notre-Dame Cathedral at **Place d'Armes**, or the foot of **Place Jacques-Cartier** in the Old Port. Sometimes there will also be a carriage waiting for you near Beaver Lake on top of **Mount Royal**. The best day for a calèche ride is any day in the morning, when most late-night revelers have yet to arrive. The best season is any season—in the warmth of summer, under the crisp autumnal sun, or snug under blankets in January. The driver's travelog is often a priceless part of this unique conveyance.

Travel the Lachine Canal★★

It is possible to travel from the Old Port to the borough of Lachine (14km/8.5mi). 514-283-6054. www.pc.gc.ca/eng/lhn-nhs/qc/canallachine/index.aspx. Open year-round daily dawn–11pm; full services available mid-May– mid-Oct. Boat tour $18. Métro Square-Victoria, orange line (Old Port) or Métro Lionel-Groulx & bus 191 (Lachine).

Pedal, ski or ride a boat through history along the Lachine Canal. It's your choice and the season's whim as to how you'll discover the historic waterway. The retired canal's been spruced up since its working days with a biking and ski trail, picnic tables, and landscaping. Along this National Historic Site, the worn brick hulks with hardwood innards have been reborn as condos. And, more

Kayaking along Lachine Canal

©Parks Canada

MUST DO

Where East is North and Local is Not Local

In Montreal, English usage (and French, for that matter) is strictly local, which is not necessarily *local* (the word for a telephone extension in Montreal). "East" and "west" are never to be taken literally (or *est* and *ouest*, for that matter). East refers to the downriver flow of the St. Lawrence River. So, depending on where you are as the river wraps around Montreal, "east" can be southeast, true east, nearly north, or, most often, northeast. Likewise, "north" means away from the St. Lawrence, which is actually toward the northwest. That means the sun can rise in the south, sort of.

recently, the locks and bridges have been repaired and upgraded.

On Two Wheels or **BIXI** – Rent a bicycle from either company at Montreal's **Old Port** and pedal into the past along the banks of the Lachine Canal. The route winds gently down, then back up at passenger and pedestrian bridges that link the two banks, and crosses the restored lock gates.

Lachine Canal Crossroads

Twelve kilometers (7.4mi) out, you'll come back to the **St. Lawrence** at the Lachine entrance. Stop at the **Lachine Canal Visitors' Centre**, straight ahead between the two locks, where outdoor signs explain the evolution of the canal. The **Lachine Museum** (1670), just to the south, holds a charming collection of local artifacts and miniature trains *(1 Chemin du Musée); 514-634-3478; open Apr–Nov Wed–Sun 11.30am–4.30pm)*. Along the north side of the canal entrance, the bicycle trail continues past the **Fur Trade at Lachine National Historic Site** *(see Museums)*.

Going Home

For more discoveries, return along Boulevard LaSalle and the St. Lawrence River. **Parc des Rapides** (Rapids Park), 5km/3mi out, is an

unexpected haven of white-water and birds in a restored marsh, and the closest you'll get to the Lachine Rapids without going over them in a raft *(514-367-6540; ville. montreal.qc.ca/grandsparcs)*.

On the Water

Most Montreal **harbor cruises★** poke into the restored lock at the eastern end of the canal before heading back out to the main channel of the river. A more leisurely cruise is available near **Atwater Market**. *For information, contact: Parks Canada, 514-283-6054; May 20–Oct 10; $18; Métro Lionel-Groulx*. Kayaks can also be rented seasonally for $5 in the same area *(514-595-6594)*, or *contact* **Lachine Canal Nautical Centre** *steps from the Atwater Market (514-842-1306 for sea kayaks, paddleboats, or even a Voyageur canoe; www.h20 adventures.ca)*.

🛶 Sauté Moutons Jet Boating and Rafting Montreal

Sauté Moutons Jet Boating, *Old Port, Clock Tower Pier. 514-284-9607. www.jetboatingmontreal.com May–Oct. $65 adults, $55 teens, $45 children. Powered ride where pioneers feared to paddle. Métro*

SPORTS AND ACTIVITIES

Jet boating the Lachine Rapids

Champ-de-Mars. **Rafting Montreal,**
8912 Boul. LaSalle. 514-767-2230.
www.raftingmontreal.com.
May–Sept. $42 adults, $37 teens,
$24 kids. Métro Angrignon, green
line, then bus 110. www.rafting
montreal.com.

You're floating down a tranquil
river one minute, and in a roiling,
drenching contest with Mother
Nature the next. You soak in rays
of sunlight, and suddenly you're
soaked in water. You're not in
the wilds of Colorado, but on the
St. Lawrence River in Montreal.
Challenge the **Lachine Rapids** in a
jet boat, or under your own steam
in a raft. It's as much fun
as a remote river trip, at a far
lower price.

Try Your Luck at Montreal Casino

Île Notre-Dame.
Access via Pont de la Concorde
(Concorde Bridge). 514-392-2746.
www.casinosduquebec.com.
Sun–Thu 9am–3am, weekends
24hr. Patrons must be at least 18
years and may be asked for photo

ID. Métro Jean-Drapeau, yellow
line, & bus 167 or free shuttle from
Dorchester Square.

Montreal's casino is proof that
sometimes governments get it
right. The casino has had to expand
several times since opening in
1992, and is currently renovating
again. It houses more than 3,000
slot machines and 120 gaming
tables, not to mention a range of
restaurants from chef Jean-Pierre
Curtat's gourmet Nuances **(AAA
5-diamond)** to moderate **Via
Fortuna, Buffet La Bonne Carte,**
and even **l'Entre Mise Deli**. Plans
are afoot to unveil a multi-platform
live perfomance venue to replace
the Broadway-style Cabaret
formerly onsite.
Games – Aside from craps, all
major games are offered, including
blackjack, slot machines, keno,
poker, roulette, and mini, midi, and
grand baccarat.
Dress Code – The casino enforces
a dress code more relaxed than it
used to be, but it prohibits bare
feet, motorcycle boots, and cutoffs.
And the drinks are *not* free.
Extras – Lottery and gambling

winnings go untaxed in Quebec. The house cut is claimed to be lower than in Las Vegas, Atlantic City, and Detroit. Valet parking and coat-check are free, and wheelchairs too.

The Building – Montreal Casino now occupies the French pavilion of the 1967 World's Fair and the adjacent Quebec pavilion. Unlike most gambling halls, it has windows, revealing spectacular views of the Montreal skyline and the St. Lawrence River.

Skating Outdoors...

Bring your skates or rent them on-site to enjoy a quintessential Montreal experience in winter. Neighborhood indoor rinks open in October, while outdoor rinks of natural ice are maintained in many parks throughout the winter. Here are a couple of choice spots to strap on skates:

Old Port★
Vieux-Port
Rue de la Commune at Boul. Saint-Laurent. 514-496-7678. www.quaysoftheoldport.com. Open early Dec–early Mar, Mon–Wed 10am–9pm, Thu–Sun 10am–10pm. $6 adults, $4 kids (under 6 free; family discounts available). Métro Place-d'Armes or Champ-de-Mars, orange line.

Skate safely right in Montreal harbor, even during the January thaw! **Bonsecours Basin** is an artificial ice surface with the river on three sides, chilled for 100 days a year. Once the St. Lawrence River freezes several feet down, you can head farther out under the watchful gaze of attendants. Skate rentals *($6)* and free lockers *(bring your own lock)* are available.

Beaver Lake in Mount Royal Park★★ Lac au Castors
Take Voie Camillien-Houde or Chemin Remembrance to the parking areas. Paid parking at Beaver Lake. 514-843-8240. www.lemontroyal.qc.ca. Park open year-round daily 6am–midnight. Métro Mont-Royal, orange line, & bus 11, or bus 166 & bus 11.
Shallow Beaver Lake freezes quickly once winter sets in, but there is an artificial zone immediately beside the Beaver Lake Chalet, and skates may be rented and sharpened onsite. There's no formality and there are no fees here. When you get cold, you can always pop upstairs to the cafeteria, or splurge and dine upscale at **Le Pavilion**, which offers one of the best restaurant **views** in the city, together with a fresh market cuisine, fine wines, and Table d'Hôte specials at lunch and dinner for $18–$25.

Atwater Market
South of the intersection of Rue Atwater & Rue Notre-Dame Ouest. 514-937-7754. www.marchespublics-mtl.com. Métro Lionel-Groulx. Under the famous clocktower Montrealers flock to their fresh produce farmer stalls, sip beverages in the continental manner, and generally take in the bounty of imported and local gourmet items at this indoor-outdoor market. To the west, the poplar-shaded bicycle trail traces the Lachine Canal towpath where workhorses once trod.

...and Skating In

L'Atrium Le 1000 de la Gauchetière

1000 Rue de la Gauchetière, between Windsor Station and Central Station. 514-395-0555. www.le1000.com.
Open throughout the year Mon–Fri 11.30am–6.00pm. Sat & Sun 10.30am–noon Tiny Tots, noon–6pm general public. $7 adults, $5 children. Métro Bonaventure, orange line.

Skate any time of the year on *the* indoor rink, under an immense glass dome. This palace of skating sits on the ground floor of "Le Mille," one of Montreal's break-the-mold office towers with a signature peaked roof. Never been on blades? No worries—lessons and rentals are available for a cost, just like the onsite parking.

Swimming Indoors...

Olympic Pool Piscine Olympique

4141 Ave. Pierre-De-Coubertin, in Olympic Park. 514-252-4141. www.rio.gouv.qc.ca. $6 adults, $4.50 children. Open year-round Mon–Fri 6.30am–10pm, weekends 9am–4.30pm. Métro Pie-IX or Viau, green line.

La Piscine Olympique is the Colosseum of pools—cavernous, skylit, with diving towers and swimming options ranging from a wading pool to one that's twice the size of a skating rink—altogether a great splash in any season. It's recommended to call first, due to training sessions.

...and Out

Notre Dame Island Beach

Île Notre-Dame. Access via Pont de la Concorde (Concorde Bridge). 514-872-6120. www.parcjeand rapeau.com. Open after Grand-Prix in Jun–late Aug daily 10am–7pm. $8 adults, $4 children.
Paddle boat and kayak rental $14/hour. Métro Jean-Drapeau, yellow line, & bus 167.

The best place for outdoor swimming *(and sailing, windsurfing, kayaking, and pedal-boating)* is at the lake on **Notre Dame Island**★, which is cleansed by plants in the adjacent lagoon. Here, the beach is sandy and you can rent almost anything you need. Free trampolines set up near the beach.

Ski in the City

Parc du Mont-Royal. Take Voie Camillien-Houde or Chemin Remembrance to the parking areas (lemontroyal.qc.ca). Métro Mont-Royal, orange line, then bus 11. Parc Nature du Cap St-Jacques, 20099, Boul. Gouin West; 514-280-6871; Métro Côte-Vertu, then bus 64, then bus 59.

Bring your cross-country skis (or snowshoes, for that matter), or rent from the onsite shops. Both locations have pay parking, food options, and plenty of room for cross-country skiing, snowshoeing, and sliding.

Mount Royal Park★★ Parc du Mont-Royal

Swish through a silent wintry wood on the fresh snow, under branches shedding a white cascade. Traverse a gentle slope, slide across

Skiing, Mount Royal Park

© Tourisme Montréal, Stéphan Poulin

a near-deserted meadow, glide around a bend, and behold the city below. This is cross-country skiing in Mount Royal Park, only minutes from most hotels.

Parc-Nature de Cap-St-Jacques Cap-Saint-Jacques Nature Park
205 Chemin du Cap-St-Jacques at Boul. Gouin, Pierrefonds. 514-280-6871. www.ville.montreal.qc.ca/grandsparcs. Métro Côte-Vertu, then bus 64, then bus 68 to the end of the line.

Head to the west of the island and through groves of maple and across creeks, with only squirrels and occasionally a fox to watch your passage.

At 267ha/659 acres, Cap St. Jacques Nature Park is the largest park on the Island of Montreal, with a historic stone château, organic farm featuring many farm animals, like cows, goats, horses, rabbits, geese, and pigs. There's a local produce boutique, plus a small eatery, picnic areas, and great beach overlooking **The Lake of Two Mountains** and the **Ottawa River**. Great spot to visit in any season. Free admission; pay parking.

⛷ Winter Carnival

Fête des Neiges
Parc Jean Drapeau, Île Ste-Hélène. Access via Pont Jacques-Cartier (Jacques-Cartier Bridge). 514-872-6120. www.parcjeandrapeau.com. Open weekends late Jan–early Feb 10am–5pm. Admission is free, fee for some activities. Métro Jean-Drapeau, yellow line, & bus 167.

It's all about oversize snowmen, toboganning down giant slides; ogling giant ice sculptures and creating smaller ones yourself; and conquering the North with a sled and a dog team. Montreal's *Fête des Neiges* is winter from the good old days, done Quebec-style, with servings of hot *poutine (french fries smothered with gravy and cheese)* and maple sugar on snow. You can rent all the equipment you'll need on-site, so there's no excuse not to join the fun. Play boot hockey, ice bockey, or just enjoy the outside winter festivities.

International Jazz Festival of Montreal

IglooFest

Come to the Jacques-Cartier Pier in Old Montreal's waterfront for nine days of electronic musical mayhem, beginning mid-Jan for three weekends, and attracting legions of hip-hop, house, electronica, and other contemporary live DJs and musicians *(514-904-1247, www.igloofest.ca)*.

🎸 Festival Fun

The city is a Mecca for great jazz perfomances in July during the annual **International Jazz Festival of Montreal** *(the largest in the world)*. Hundreds of free concerts outside complement the packed indoor itinerary of jazz, rock, blues, gypsy, and other styles as well. Also features the popular three-day **Salon de Guitare** with global artisans, workshops, and speakers. **Festival Juste-Pour-Rire (Just For Laughs Festival)** holds court throughout the city during July. The icons of comedy flock here to perform, sign TV contracts, and share new routines.
For details about festivals, see Calendar of Events.

Free Entertainment

Mix with the crowds and join in the applause around a fire-eater, a team of jugglers, or a unicyclist on Rue Jeanne-Mance or anywhere in and around **Place des Arts** during the Jazz Fest. Roar at the edgy antics of an up-and-coming comedy duo on a lane off **Rue Saint-Denis** during the Just for Laughs Festival, or join in the circus arts fun at **Complétement Cirque**, where circus acts from around the world perform at numerous venues across the city.

Festival Tents

Local laws are relaxed during the Jazz Fest, the High Lights Festival, and whenever people gather for a recognized street event. Pick up a paper cup of good Canadian beer from the sponsoring brewery, and while you're at it, banter with the locals who have come downtown for the event, along with visitors from all over.

FOR KIDS

Montreal has museums for kids, festivals for kids, and an amusement park almost in the middle of town. *C'est le fun!* **Responsible youngsters just might wonder whether there's enough for their parents to do.**

Montreal Insectarium★
Insectarium de Montréal

4581 Rue Sherbrooke Est, on the grounds of the Montreal Botanical Garden. 514-872-1400. www2.ville.montreal.qc.ca/ insectarium. Open daily in summer, 9am–6pm; mid-Sept–Oct Tue– Sun 9am–9pm; rest of the year Tue–Sun 9am–5pm. $14 winter, $16.50 summer (includes Botanical Garden). Métro Pie-IX, green line, or bus 185; or take the free shuttle from Viau Métro.

Local legend Georges Brossard, affectionately know worldwide as the "Bug Man" convinced the Montreal mayor bugs were sadly misunderstood. For many years, Brossard had been collecting hundreds of species, but no one else was sharing his bounty. After an impressive fundraising event in 1987, Brossard donated his entire collection, and the Insectarium was born. The public has passionately supported this venue ever since. The folks at the Insectarium are just full of tidbits of arthropod information But they're more than just talk. They'll lead you through a cloud of monarch butterflies

flapping softly against your skin, and on to sturdy, state-of-the-art greenhouses where insects from around the globe fly and hop about. In summer, you'll walk through gardens that are planted precisely to attract creepy-crawlies. Homely, invisible or gorgeous, insects are part of our world, and the Insectarium gives them their rightful place, in the food chain, the environment, controlling pests, looking after the dirty work, and sometimes just being downright pesky. Try a sample to eat even!

Busy Bodies ant hill exhibit

© Montréal Insectarium/Florin Feneru

Ice Skating at L'Atrium

1000 Rue de la Gauchetière, between Windsor Station and Central Station. 514-395-0555. www.le1000.com. Open throughout the year Mon–Fri 11am–6pm, Sat/ Sun 10.30–noon "Tiny Tots" program, and from noon–6pm general public. Métro Bonaventure, orange line. It's what Montreal kids do, or the child in any adult, too. Get out on the ice and skate. Skate all year under the dome at L'Atrium. No skates? Rent a pair. No experience? Take a lesson. Primary goal? Have fun!

Mission Gaia, Montreal Science Centre

Montréal Science Centre (iSci)★
Centre des Sciences de Montréal

King-Edward Pier, Old Port (Boul. 333 Rue de la Commune at the foot of Boul. Saint-Laurent). 514-496-4724. www.montrealsciencecentre. com. Open mid-Jun daily 10am–5pm; mid-Jun–early Sept Sun–Thu 10am–9pm & Fri–Sat 10am–9pm. Rest of the year Mon–Fri 9am–5pm & Sat 10am–9pm, Sun 10am–6pm. $11.50 or $19 for two IMAX tickets, (discounts available for children and families). Métro Place d'Armes, orange line.

The "i" in iSci stands for "interactive," and this see-through steel-and-glass greenhouse is all about taking control of the science experience through computers and wizardry. **idTV** recreation of a real television newsroom gives kids a first-hand feel for what is involved; research a topic, discuss it with your partners, compile the data, edit the video, and host the report yourself. Random picks could see your work broadcast on the center's big

screen "**Special News Flash**." **IMAX** films take you right into the action on a curving, oversize screen. Enjoy such movies as *Born To Be Wild*, or *U23D*, as sensational experiences or for their scientific content, or (preferably) both. Travelogues and seasonal specials (*Santa vs the Snowman*) are regular features. English and French soundtracks alternate. **Eureka Festival** – Explore health, your everyday environment, and strange-but-true physical forces through games, multimedia challenges, and access to the world's top scientific experts. **Mission Gaia** Play alone or in a team of two to four people. Players are faced with environmental situations, such as some of our real-world puzzles in the 20C.

La Ronde★

22 Chemin MacDonald, Parc Jean Drapeau, Île Ste-Hélène. 514-397-2000. www.laronde.com. Open mid–late May weekends 10am–8pm, late May–mid-Jun 10am–8pm, mid-Jun–Aug 10am–

10.30pm; Sept–Oct weekends & holidays noon–7 or 8pm (from 10am Labor Day weekend). $40 adults, $25 children under 137cm/54in. Parking: $15. Métro Jean Drapeau, then bus 167.

The largest amusement center in Eastern Canada, La Ronde enjoys a prime location on **St. Helen's Island** (Île Ste-Hélène) in the St. Lawrence River, opposite downtown. Give your teens Métro tickets and admission money, and let them loose on Vertigo, Vampire, Le Monstre, Cobra, Boomerang, L'Orbite, or Goliath.

Attractions have been climbing higher and spinning faster since Six Flags took over the park, and La Ronde has gone from a charming, city-owned installation and part of Expo-67 World's Fair, to the big leagues of summer fun.

If thrill rides aren't your thing, try the tamer log-flume and bumper cars. The truly motion-shy can opt for concerts, magicians, and street entertainers at a reduced admission rate. And there's no better vantage point for the World Fireworks Competition in summer than La Ronde; the Pont Jacques-Cartier *(Jacques Cartier Bridge)* is closed 8pm to the end.

🎪 Festival Fun for Kids

Who said the Jazz Fest was only for grown-ups? Great big inflatable slides and games are set up in **Place des Arts** every afternoon during the festival. Clowns are out painting faces, and there go the acrobats piling atop each other on **Rue Jeanne-Mance**, and a unicyclist riding backward while he juggles. And did you see the fire-eater? One of the most popular attractions is the daily New Orleans-style **Parade de Festival**, winding its way through the festival grounds and attracting all ages to follow the march of the musicians.

During the **Just for Laughs Festival**, a crowd of acts and jokesters perform on the streets in the **Latin Quarter**. They speak three languages—English, French, and/or pantomime—and of course, kids are better at getting the joke than anyone else, even if they don't understand every word.

Festivals Just for Kids

The **Children's Festival** *(La Fête des enfants)* festival draws 100,000 participants to **Parc Jean Drapeau** in August to rides and free access to the **Biosphère Canada** site. Native dances, concerts of Quebec music, trampolines, water events, and most are free.
For details: 514-872-0060 or www.ville.parcjeandrapeau.com.
TOHU *(2345 Rue Jarry East)* is the acclaimed international center for

©Richard Nowitz/Apa Publications

La Ronde

121

Street Fun

Even if there's no festival during your visit, there is always plenty of street fun in Montreal. Head to **Place Jacques-Cartier** in Old Montreal, or right down to the **Old Port**, where face-painters, balloon-twisting artists, sword-swallowers, and performers of a dozen arts and entertainments vie for your attention, your hearts, and your spare change.

circus arts training, production, and performance. It has an amazing, ongoing program of events for children, many of which are free. *www.tohu.ca.*

Labyrinthe du Hangar 16, in an authentic Old Port waterside warehouse, offers kids and parents a challenging thematic maze to try to pass through. *$15 adults, $11.50 kids, and various group deals listed on website or call 514-499-0099 (www.labyrintheduhangar16.com).*

Winter Carnival *(Fête des Neiges)* sees grown-ups pushed aside by kids racing to the toboggan and tube slides. *See For Fun.*

Excursions for Fun

🚀 The Cosmodôme★★

2150 Laurentian Autoroute, Laval. 12km/7mi north of Montreal via Hwy. 15 to Exit Boul. Saint-Martin. 450-978-3600. www.cosmodome.org. Open Sep–June Tue–Sun 10am–5pm; summer daily 10am-5pm. Métro Montmorency, orange line, then bus 70 or 61. $11.50 adults, $7.50 children (self-guided visit).

Take a grand tour of the solar system throughout its turbulent history. Learn how space and space science work magic on farming, mining, communications, and surveillance.

Videos, sound effects, and computer-controlled lighting enhance the experience. The **Parent-Child Discovery Camp** is an overnight adventure of the imagination in a space console. Cosmodôme's **Endeavor Camp** is a week-long adventure for prospective young astronauts, using a duplicate of the Endeavor shuttle and other simulators.

The Cosmodôme

Exporail

110 Rue Saint-Pierre, St-Constant. 20km/12mi south of Montreal. Take Autoroute 15 crossing the Champlain Bridge South to Hwy. 132 West, then go south on Hwy. 209 or Rue Saint-Pierre. 450-632-2410. www.exporail.org. Open 10am–5pm and until 6pm during peak summer, June–Sep. $17 adults, $11 children (ages 13-17), $8 children under 13.

Steam locomotives and passenger cars of times gone by are on display at the Canadian Railway Museum, and some of them are even living productive second lives. Forty-five of the greatest oldies are lovingly cared for and sheltered indoors. Treasures include the opulent private car of Canadian Pacific Railway magnate William Van Horne, the oldest steam locomotive built in Canada, and Montreal's first electric streetcar, the Rocket. Guided tours aboard some of the precious antiques take place at 2.30pm on weekends. On Sundays you can ride a vintage locomotive for a kilometre or two through the countryside.

Mont Saint-Saveur Parc Aquatique

350 Rue Saint-Denis, Saint-Saveur-des-Monts. Take Laurentian Autoroute 15 north to Exit 58, then signs for Mont-Saint-Saveur. Open May to Labor Day 11am–4pm until 7pm in summer. $33 over age 13, $25 under age 13. 450-227-4671. www.parcaquatique.com.

When summer heat arrives in Quebec, the humidity drives many up the Laurentian Autoroute to this water park for cooling relief: water slides, rafting, coasters, lazy river rides, camping, and even surfing

the waves. Packages can combine camping or even nearby hotels. Don't miss the **Acro-Nature** option offering over 305m/1,000ft of elevated mobile beams, accordion foot briges, timber ladders, and zip-lines. Or the **Alpine-Coaster**, a dizzying summer toboggan run through a mountainous, forested course for almost an hour, sure to delight. Both Acro-Nature and Alpine-Coaster are an added cost.

Whale Bus Express

Croisiéres AML, 1-800-563-4643, from early July until after Labor Day, $159 kids age 2–16, $169 adults (supper included). www.croisieresaml.com.

If you are visiting Quebec for the first time, treat yourself and the kids to viewing some of the best wildlife anywhere. This unique one-day bus/boat tour from the **Centre InfoTouristique** at Dorchester Square *(1255 Rue Peel)* to the riveside community of Riviére-de-Loup, and aboard the Cavalier des Mers, brings you to the habitat of three species of whales inhabiting the waters of the mighty St. Lawrence River.

Grande Bibiliothèque de Montreal l'Éspace Jeunes

475 Boul. de Maisonneuve Est, corner Rue Berri. Métro Berri-UQAM, 514-873-1100. www.banq.qc.ca.

The entire lower level of this library is dedicated to kids. The colorful media zone features half-moon couches with video screens, where you listen to music, watch movies, or play games.

FOR KIDS

BOX OFFICE

PERFORMING ARTS

With an expanded Place des Arts complex, the new Quartier des Spectacles entertainment district, and TOHU's Cité des Arts du Cirque, Montreal has more first-rate performance venues than ever before.

⚜ Place des Arts★★

175 Rue Sainte-Catherine Ouest. 514-842-2112. www.laplacedes arts.com. Open daily and for performances. Métro Place des Arts or Saint-Laurent, green line. See Landmarks.

That's "Plaza of the Arts," and no name is more accurate, especially now with a new **Montreal Symphony Hall** for the Montreal Symphony Orchestra to perform in. Montreal's premier locale for live entertainment consists of four structures bordering a central square: a concert hall, a theater building, the **Montreal Contemporary Art Museum★★** *(see Museums)*, and the symphony hall. The plaza hosts everything from opera to Broadway musicals, ballet, film festivals, and outdoor events. It also acts as the main hub for the international **Jazz Festival of Montreal, Francofolies Festival**, etc.

Venues and Virtuosos

Salle Wilfrid-Pelletier is home to the **Orchestre Symphonique** (Montreal Symphony Orchestra, or MSO), the **Opéra de Montréal**, and **Les Grands Ballets Canadien**, as well as host to major touring shows. **Théâtre Jean-Duceppe** has its own company. **Théâtre Maisonneuve** is a large, multipurpose hall. Also here are the smaller **Studio Théâtre** and **Théâtre Café de la Place**.

Resident Companies

- **L'Opéra de Montréal**, *260 Rue de Maisonneuve, 514-985-2252. www.operademontreal.com.*
- **Orchestre Symphonique de Montréal**, *514-842-9951. www.osm.ca.*
- **Compagnie Jean-Duceppe**, *514-842-2112. www.duceppe.com* Live theater in French.
- **Orchestre Métropolitain du Grand Montréal**, *514-598-0870. www.orchestremetropolitain.com.*

Place des Arts

©Gregory B. Gallagher/Michelin

MUST DO

BOX OFFICE

Tickets, not TKTS

Where to book your tickets for entertainment in Montreal? You probably don't want to spend your valuable travel time running from window to window (and hoping they're open). Fortunately, you can make arrangements by phone or through the Web. You can also call or visit **La Vitrine** *(145 Rue Sainte-Catherine West, 514-285-4545, www.lavitrine.com)* for all your **last-minute ticket** needs, as well as access to most cultural events, in or around the city.

♦ For **Place des Arts**, go to www.placedesarts.com, click on "Show" and then the "Tickets" link; call 514-842-2112 or 866-842-2112; or visit the box office *(entrance off Rue Ste-Catherine; open Mon–Sat 10am–9pm).*

♦ For many other venues and shows, you can purchase tickets at **Envenko** *(www.evenko.ca, 514-790-2525)*, **TicketPro** *(www.ticketpro.ca 514-908-9090)* or **Admission** *(www.admission.com, 514-790-1245)*. Many venues, as well as festivals such as the **Jazz Fest** and **FrancoFolies**, sell tickets through these major outlets.

Montreal's other main orchestra performs in Place des Arts, St. John the Baptist Church *(Rue Sainte-Catherine east of Rue Bleury)*, and free at Théâtre de Verdure in La Fontaine Park *(see Parks and Gardens)*.

THEATERS

🎭 Centre Bell (Bell Centre)
1260 Rue de la Gauchetière Ouest. 514-790-2525. www.centrebell.ca. Métro Bonaventure, orange line.
When Montreal's hockey palace isn't hosting the legendary *Les Canadiens*, it stages rock concerts featuring stars too popular for performances at Place des Arts. Occasionally, even the Bell Centre will prove insufficient and a show will book the **Olympic Stadium** in **Olympic Park★★**.

Centaur Theatre
453 Rue Saint-François-Xavier. 514-288-3161. www.centaurtheatre.com. Métro Place-d'Armes, orange line.
Montreal's main English-language theater legacy presents Broadway, off-Broadway, and Canadian shows

in their intimate halls built into the former quarters of the Montreal Stock Exchange historical building in Old Montreal.

Centre Pierre-Peladeau
300 Boul. de Maisonneuve Est. 514-987-4691. www.centrepierre peladeau.uqam.ca. Métro Berri-UQAM.
One of Montreal's newer live-performance centers, bequeathed by (and named after) a newspaper magnate, operates in cooperation

Théâtrical Café-Sitting

If you miss the performance at Théâtre du Nouveau Monde, there's always another show of intellectual debate and animated discussion in its **Café du Nouveau Monde**. Keep your eyes and ears open in the upstairs restaurant, or the cafe-bar that overflows to the sidewalk in warmer weather. The fare is French and bistro European, and you can order anything from a beverage only to fresh tuna carpaccio or merguez couscous.

PERFORMING ARTS

Cinema Out of the Ordinary

ex-Centris/Cinema Parallele – 3536 Boul. St-Laurent. 514-847-2206. www.cinema-parallele.ca. $11 general admission, matinee before 6pm $8.50 (Mon–Fri) , kids under 12 yrs $6, students & 60+ $8. Monday Special $8.50. Métro St-Laurent, green line. The ex-Centris legacy may now add the salvaging of one of the city's dearly beloved independent theaters to their list of new media accomplishments. Software mogul Daniel Langlois took his millions and invested them where his heart was to build a cinema and a new media complex into and around pre-existing neighborhood commercial structures. Even if you're not in town for a movie, stop by ex-Centris for a look at the movie-going experience as it could be. The mandate here is to support film making not seen at the chains. Langlois' company's original **Fellini** and **Cassavetes** venues have been remodeled to welcome Cinema Parallele film fans. The balance of the building continues to nurture original, independent media arts experimentation across a wide menu of styles. They have also added live musicians and performances to their roster, so call before to check current events. Onsite **Café Meliés** (514-847-9218) serves excellent fare.

with the Department of Music at Université du Québec à Montréal (aka UQAM). This Latin-Quarter location includes ultra-sleek, state-of-the-art **Salle Pierre-Mercure**. Jazz, classical music, dance, world music, and lectures are all on the program, and some Saturday-afternoon events are free.

Segal Centre Performing Arts

5170 Chemin de la Côte-Ste-Catherine. 514-739-2301. www.segalcentre.org. Métro Côte Sainte-Catherine, orange line. Designed by Phyllis Lambert as the **Saiyde Bronfman Centre**, honoring her mother and matriarch, is now home to Segal Theatre, Academy of Performing Arts, CinemaSpace, Studio, and the Dora Wasserman Yiddish Theatre.

Théâtre du Nouveau Monde

84 Rue Sainte-Catherine Ouest. 514-866-8668. www.tnm.qc.ca. Métro Place-des-Arts or St.Laurent.

The "New World Theatre" opened in 1912 as **The Gaiety** for vaudeville, changed to a striptease joint (Lili St-Cyr danced here), and once served as a cinema. Now it's been lovingly restored and features French-language theatrical premieres (Robert Lepage, etc.), plus Shakespeare and contemporary playwrights adapted into French, plus festival music performances.

Théâtre Saint-Denis

1594 Rue Saint-Denis. 514-849-4211. www.theatrestdenis.com. Métro Berri-UQAM. Two halls. Théâtre St-Denis is the place to see French-language music-hall shows, popular singers, and **Just for Laughs Festival** galas.

Théâtre de Verdure

In Parc La Fontaine, Rue Sherbrooke at Ave. Parc-La Fontaine. 514-872-2644. Métro Sherbrooke, orange line or Métro Papineau green line. Montreal's free outdoor summer theater performance venue fits

MUST DO

into a natural bowl, with plenty of seating. Classical music, Shakespeare *(English, too),* and dance recitals by major companies are presented on summer nights. *Over 50 free events each season.*

Festivals of the Arts

In Montreal, the whole city's a stage for classical music and jazz, live theater, and more. Check out the **Calendar of Events** at the beginning of this guide to find out what's happening when you're in town. Here's a taste of festival fare:

February

Festival en Lumière – Chefs, foodies, and artisans hold court throughout the city in a global food festival featuring workshops, tastings, nightly fireworks, and special chef duets at local eateries.

May

Festival TransAmériques – The best and the most promising contemporary theater and dance companies from all over the hemisphere gather and perform in Montreal.

Chamber Music Festival – Performances are given at the chalet in **Mount Royal Park**, in the streets of **Old Montreal**, and at the **Bon-Pasteur Chapel**.

June

Saint Ambroise Fringe Festival If it's daring and it's theater, it's in the Fringe Festival in the **Plateau Mont-Royal** district.

July

Festival International de Jazz de Montréal – The greatest and the undiscovered names in jazz, blues, rock, raggae, and more converge on the Place des Arts area.

Festival International de Lanaudière – The must-see summer festival for classical music takes place in the community of Joliette, northeast of Montreal.

Nuits d'Afrique – Sultry rhythms and tropical beats take over multiple stages.

Les FrancoFolies – The melodies and lyrics of French composers will make you laugh or move you to tears, even if you don't understand a word.

October

Festival International de Nouvelle Danse – The borders between dance, ballet, and acrobatics disappear.

Orgue et couleurs – The organ is the centerpiece in concerts at various religious venues throughout the city.

November

Coup de Coeur Francophone – Celebrate the art of the *chanson*, the best in French lyrics.

Festival International de Jazz de Montréal

© Jean Heguy/age fotostock

PERFORMING ARTS

127

NIGHTLIFE

Montreal by night is exotic, forbidden, edgy, but always entertaining. These qualities are at the city's very historical core, from running bootleg booze during American Prohibition to becoming an entertainment hub during the Recording Blackout of the 1940s, to after-hours joints, to commonly accepted strip clubs. Visitors flock here knowing the *joie-de-vivre* is contagious, especially after midnight.

Venues

L'Astral/Bistro Balmoral (Maison du Festival RioTinto Alcan)

305 Rue Sainte-Catherine West, 514-288-5992, Métro Place-des-Arts, green line. l'Astral open for live shows (check website), Le Balmoral open 11am–11pm for dining & shows. www.montreal jazzfestival.com.

The closing of the venerable **Le Spectrum** gave rise to the opening of a new cultural center in the renovated **Blumenthal Building** across the street, now called **Maison du Festival RioTinto Alcan**. L'Astral, designed with the old music palace in mind, seats 600 in a more intimate two-story live setting. Meanwhile, **Le Balmoral** at ground level, with a **view** over the new **Quartier-des-Spectacles** festival landscape, allows visitors and locals alike to support the non-profit eatery and free outdoor festival concerts. Local live jazz and blues is regularly featured. A boutique at ground level offers visitors festival souvenirs, while upstairs you'll find **Galerie Lounge TD**, with traveling photography exhibitions, plus a permanent collection of artwork by Miles Davis, Tony Bennett, and many others. The third floor **Mediathéque Jazz** is a unique jazz resource center.

Café Campus

57 Rue Prince-Arthur Est, Plateau Mont-Royal. 514-844-1010. Métro Sherbrooke, orange line, or Métro Saint-Laurent, green line. www.cafecampus.com.

One of Montreal's favorite night-clubs is located in the liveliest section of the **Plateau Mont-Royal** district. Pedestrian-only **Rue Prince-Arthur** is a show in itself at all hours year-round. Steady lineup of international and local acts.

Club Balattou

4372 Boul. Saint-Laurent, Plateau Mont-Royal. 514-845-5447. www.nuitsdafrique.com. Métro Saint-Laurent, green line, then 55 bus.

Fashioned after venues like Club Balattou in Paris or Marseilles: pulsing rhythms from numerous tropical countries thrive here. Local musicians and international names from Senegal, Martinique, Guadeloupe, and the Congo.

Ernie Butler's Comedy Nest

2313 Rue Sainte-Catherine West, at Atwater. 514-932-6378. www.thecomedynest.com. Métro Atwater, green line.

Ernie Butler started the city's first comedy club called Stitches. Thirty years later, and 7,000 shows to the club's credit, English-language performers from everywhere hold court on the third floor in the Pepsi Forum.

Upstairs Jazz Bar

1254 Rue McKay, east of Rue Guy. 514-931-6808. Métro Guy-Concordia, green line. Open Mon–Thu 11am–1am, Fri until 2am, Sat 5.30pm–2am, Sun 6.30–1am. www.upstairsjazz.com.

This is Montreal's classic jazz club, and a social meeting hub for journeyman musicians, novices, or nearby Concordia students alike. Small quarters make the **Upstairs**—which is not upstairs— an intimate, easy-going lair, where musicians chat easily with patrons between sets and over food.

House of Jazz

2060 Rue Aylmer, Downtown. 514-842-8656. Métro McGill, green line.

Jazz rules in Montreal. Oscar Peterson was born and raised here, and for years Charles Biddle ran this establishment under his own name.

Crescent Street

Métro Guy-Concordia, green line.

Located between **Rue Sherbrooke** and **Boul. Rene-Levesque**, parallel to **Rue de la Montagne** lies a party zone street of bistros, pubs, and eateries patronized for decades by the Who's Who of the sports, entertainment, and society pages. Check into the **Hard Rock Café** (no. 1458) for a familiar combo of Rock & Roll memorabilia, a huge dance floor, plus Cajun dishes. While on this famous street, go across to the **Sir Winston Churchill Pub** (no. 1459) to mix with the local pub crew, or the rooftop terrace at **Le Newtown** (no. 1476), or the popular dancefloor at **Thursdays** (no. 1449), along one of English Montreal's late-night party blocks.

Cabaret Bistro Lion d'Or

1676 Rue Ontario East, 514-598-0709. www.cabaretliondor.com.

Fabulous live music venue, bistro, and attached eatery **Au Petit Extra**, with great lunch and dinner.

Le St-Sulpice

1680 Rue St-Denis, Latin Quarter. 514-844-9458. Métro Berri-UQAM.

Beer, dancing, and live music or a DJ are the attractions in every nook and cranny on three floors of this classic French-Canadian town house. The *terrasses* are staked out early in summer. Lines can be lengthy at this prime nightspot on the *rue*, but the host of clubs north on **Rue St-Denis** past **Rue Sherbrooke** absorb the overflow.

La Sala Rosa/Casa del Popolo

4848 & 4873 Boul. Saint-Laurent, Métro Saint-Laurent, then 55 bus, 514-284-0122. Open various times. www.suoniperilpopolo.com.

Experimental music, poetry, and performance lives here. Continuous international and local lineup of sounds off the main grid; unique, and not necessarily for tapping your feet. **Paul Robeson** and **Eleanor Roosevelt** spoke up for workers' rights here and this 1930s building built by the Jewish-Left Movement continues to be a community center.

SHOPPING

Start with a Canadian dollar that can drop against its US counterpart. Add Quebec fashion flair and a range of quality local products from maple syrup to soapstone carvings. Stir in extraordinary know-how in the design of retail emporia and you've got a recipe for shopping, shopping, and more shopping. Stores are generally open Mon–Wed 9am–6 or 7pm, Thu–Fri 9am–9pm, Sat 10am–5pm, and Sun noon–5pm, with extended hours before Christmas.

Marché Bonsecours

350 Rue St-Paul Est. 514-872-7730. www.marchebonsecours.qc.ca. Open summer daily, 10am–9pm; Apr–summer Sat–Wed 10am–6pm, Thu & Fri 10am–9pm; Labor Day–Oct Sun–Wed 10am–6pm, Thu–Sat 10am–9pm; Jan–Mar 10am–6pm. Métro Champ-de-Mars, orange line. See Historic Sites.

The old market in Old Montreal is not just a historic site, it's a gathering of some of the leaders in design. The Galérie des Métiers d'Art is a fine crafts exhibition center, as well as a shop. Items available elsewhere in the building include Inuit soapstone carvings and Native Canadian crafts; blown glass (with on-site demonstrations)

at Studio gogo glass, and prêt-à-porter (ready-to-wear) fashions.

Rue Crescent★

Around the intersection of Rue Crescent with Rue Sainte-Catherine you'll find the "labels," from home-grown Parasuco to ALDO, Guess, Benetton, and Canadian icon Roots. Stores in this "hood" are constantly in heavy sales competition, so buyers have the upper hand.

🚶 Rue Saint-Denis

From Rue Sherbrooke to Rue Duluth. If there's a new twist to anything, you'll find it on Rue Saint-Denis in the **Plateau Mont-Royal** section just north of Rue Sherbrooke and the Latin Quarter. This neighborhood has the highest concentration of residents who do NOT own a car in North America; students, artists, and entrpreneurs, but you will still find some of leading-edge clothing, jewelry, bread, soap, and furniture designers here.

Downtown Department and Fashion Stores

Les Ailes de la Mode
677 Rue Sainte-Catherine Ouest. 514-282-4537. www.lesailes.com. Part of the former Eaton's department store is now a high-end emporium of eye-

---

Gourmet Gifts

Maple syrup and smoked salmon are mainstays at hotel gift shops, but you'll find a more varied assortment of gourmet products at **Chez l'Epicier**, across from Bonsecours Market *(311 Rue St-Paul Est; 514-878-2232; www.chezlepicier.com)*. House specialties include award-winning maple syrup flavored with rum or blueberries, and smoked lamb, duck, and bison.

MUST DO

Public Markets

For the fun of shopping alongside locals, head for Montreal's public markets. Outdoor stands overflow with produce during mild weather and the indoor shops of Montreal's markets remain busy every day of the year. www.marchepublics-mtl.com.

Atwater Market *(see Musts for Fun)* has ingredients for French cuisine, exotic coffees, and hand-made chocolates, as well as Latin American and West Indian food. **Jean Talon Market★★** *(Métro Jean Talon, orange line)* in Montreal's Little Italy features cured and packaged delicacies that reflect English, French, Italian, and Native American traditions: maple products (including maple ice wine), venison, buffalo, and Brome Lake duck. **Marché Saint-Jacques**: Rue Ontario East at Rue Amherst is a newbie.

catching fashion. Some of the cherished Art-Deco features of the former occupant remain.

La Baie
Rue Sainte-Catherine at Ave. Union. 514-281-4422. www.hbc.com.
A Canadian institution, this downtown department store lives on in Montreal as "La Baie" *(short for Compagnie de la Baie d'Hudson, or Hudson's Bay Company)*. Hudson's Bay blankets are for many the emblem of the North. Look inside for gifts, delicacies, and everything else with a Canadian slant.

Birks
1240 Phillips-Square, opposite La Baie. 514-297-2511. www.birks.com.
This long-established luxury jewelry store occupies a place comparable to Tiffany's in New York, but it's more affordable. Check out the window displays at the very least and enjoy the new Afternoon Tea onsite at **Café by Europea**.

Ogilvy's
1307 Rue Sainte-Catherine Ouest. 514-842-7711. www.ogilvycanada.com.
Legendary department store,

where a Scottish bagpipes player marches through in the afternoon. Once an upscale department store in its own right, it's now a collection of name-brand boutiques, maintaining heritage fixtures and many traditions, including the irresistible Christmas window display.

Simons
977 Rue Sainte-Catherine Ouest. 514-282-1840. www.somins.ca.
High-quality, down-to-earth prices and styling with flair are characteristics of this Quebec City store, which took Montreal *(and the former Simpson's department store)* by storm a few years ago.

Underground City
Place Montreal-Trust, Eaton Centre, Promenades de la Cathédrale, Place VilleMarie . See map pp 56–57.
On a day that's too cold or too hot for the outdoors, or simply because there are so many must-buys in Montreal, head to one of the shopping complexes that connect via the Underground City. Unlike some of the other retailers, Eaton Centre is *open until 9pm (Mon–Fri).*

SHOPPING

131

Mega Malls

Canada invented the "strip mall" and embraced, refined, and perfected the indoor suburban shopping mall, with several vast examples within easy Métro reach of downtown Montreal.

Carrefour Angrignon

7077 Boul. Newman, La Salle. www.carrefourangrignon.com. Métro Angrignon, green line.
Located in the southwestern **La Salle** neighborhood, Carrefour Angrignon serves a mixed English- and French-speaking area, with stores ranging from Sears to Gap to Canadian Tire *(a hardware icon)* and a discount supermarket.

Place Versailles

7275 Rue Sherbrooke Est. 514-353-5940. www.placeversailles.com. Métro Radisson, orange line.
The largest mall in the region has 225 stores, ranging from a branch of department store La Baie to Quebec-only labels to **Bikini Village**, to a one-of-a-kind coin dealer and the ever-present lottery counter. The location is perfect for a shopping outing after a ball game at **Olympic Stadium** or a visit to the **Insectarium** *(see For Kids)* and the **Botanical Garden** *(see Parks and Gardens)*, both of which have great boutiques for gifts.

Museum Shops

Yes, there are T-shirts in museum boutiques, but also one-of-a-kind items you won't find elsewhere. *No museum admission is required.*

Musée d'Art Contemporain

(Montreal Contemporary Art Museum), 185 Rue Sainte-Catherine Ouest. 514-847-6226. See Museums.
The shop here is accessible, in keeping with the museum's mission of modern-art outreach. Jewelry by local artists is featured.

Pointe-à-Callière Museum

(Montreal Museum of Archaeology and History), 350 Place-Royale at Rue de la Commune. See Museums.
You'll find an excellent selection of wood and metal crafts, blown glass, fine jewelry, books, and art.

Musée des Beaux-Arts

(Montreal Museum of Fine Arts), 1380 Rue Sherbrooke Ouest. 514-285-2000. See Museums.
The museum shop features catalogs of current exhibitions and prints, and limited-edition household wares and fine handmade crafts from the far corners of the world, or local artisans.

Neighborhoods for Shopping

The Fur District

Politically incorrect though it may be, the commerce that built Montreal lives on. Most fur garments in Canada are crafted by hand in commercial buildings throught the city. **Rue Bleury** and **Rue Mayor** in the eastern part of downtown have quite a few. If you're lucky, you might even see pelts being sorted and graded. **Here's a sampling of showrooms: Alexandor Furs** – *6570 Rue Saint-Hubert. 514-288-1119. www.alexandorfurs.com.*

Something Old

Rue Notre-Dame, from Rue Atwater to Rue Guy. Montreal just oozes old furniture, furnishings and fittings at prices that attract antique dealers from New England and abroad. Browse the shops along Rue Notre Dame for pine tables, classic bathroom fittings, and stained-glass windows dating back to the 19C. Furniture of the French regime is hard to find, but excellent reproductions are available on **Rue St-Paul** in Old Montreal, and in **Bonsecours Market.**

Grossman Furs – *9250 Ave. du Parc. 514-288-3239. www.samuelgross manfurs.com.*
Hercules Furs – *350 Rue Mayor. 514 -842-2492. www.herculesfurs.com.*
McComber – *9250 Ave. du Parc. 514-845-1167.*
Mega Furs – *397 Rue Mayor. 514-844-8651.*
North Pole Furs – *366 Rue Mayor. 514-842-7969. www.north polefurs.com.*

Gallery Row
Rue Sherbrooke, west of Rue Crescent.
This is the legendary "Golden Mile District" around the Museum of Fine Arts and also prime territory for sourcing paintings by contemporary Quebec and Canadian artists. Browse the windows on both sides of **Rue Sherbrooke**, west of the museum.

Outremont
Sedate, classy, well-off ... that's Outremont, the crème de la crème of French-speaking neighborhoods in Montreal *(see Neighborhoods)*. A famous theater, pastry shops, boutiques, specialty cheese shops, bistros, and dining rooms can easily absorb a full day of browsing.

Avenue Laurier
West of Boul. Saint-Laurent, Métro Laurier, orange line.
Along Outremont's main commercial thoroughfare you can acquire body potions at the flagship boutique of Quebec's own **Lise Watier** *(no. 392; 514-270-9296; www.lisewatier.com).* **Jet-Setter** *(no. 66; 514-271-5058)* is an amazing store for travelers, with clothes, luggage, tools, maps, and a cornucopia of other goodies.

Cuban Rum and Cigars

US customs officials at Montreal airports and the border are ever on the alert for these items.

Havana Club rum is available in any bar, or by the bottle in provincial liquor outlets (branded SAQ, or Societé des Alcools du Québec). Cuban cigars are less widely available, but are stocked by specialty tobacco shops, such as **Casa del Habano** *(1434 Rue Sherbrooke Ouest; 514-849-0037; www.lacasadelhabano.com).*

SHOPPING

SPAS

Montrealers thrive on living life with abandon, but just count the number of businesses around town dedicated to nurturing body, mind, and spirit, and you will see a system at work in *la belle province*.

Atmosphère

475 Ave. President-Kennedy, in the Delta Montreal Hotel, Downtown. 514-284-4357. www.atmosphere spa.qc.ca. Métro McGill, green line. Open daily; Mon–Fri 9am–9pm, Sat/Sun 10am–9pm.

Atmosphère is conveniently located inside the **Hotel Delta Montreal**, enabling the spa to complement its treatment offerings with the hotel's pool, sauna, and whirlpool. Mainstays are massage treatments, balneotherapy, algae wraps, and body peels. *Packages range from a choice of one treatment paired with a 30-minute massage, a two-day menu of pampering, or their special couples pack.*

Rainspa

55 Rue Saint-Jacques Ouest in the Hotel Place d'Armes, Old Montreal. 514-282-2727. Métro Place d'Armes, orange line. Open Mon–Sat 9am–8pm, Sun 9am–7pm.

Rainspa, on the third floor of the **Hotel Place d'Armes**, offers Swedish, hot stone, aromatherapy, and shower massages, along with body treatments. All packages include access to the **hammam**, Montreal's only Middle-Eastern steam bath. Ask about the Urban Getaway Special.

Aveda Spa & Academy

3613 Boul. St-Laurent. 514-499-9494. www.avedamontreal-lifestyle.com. Métro Sherbrooke, orange line. Open daily 10am. Closed Monday.

First combo in Canada by this international brand on the former site of Salon Tonic features a professional Aveda Academy, plus lifestyle salon and spa. Splurge a little or a little more than usual on their **Nirvana Special**: a 1hr massage starts this journey to bliss, then an **Elemental Nature 90min facial** sends you into the zone, after which you come out to have your hair coiffed and nails manicured. All this includes lunch, in a super relaxed ambiance.

Bota Bota

©Bota Bota / Sid Lee

MUST DO

Destination: Spa Eastman

895 Chemin des Diligences, Eastman. 110km/69mi east of Montreal via Autoroute 10; take Exit 106 and follow signs in the village of Eastman. 450-297-3009 or 800-665-5272. www.spa-eastman.com.

©Spa Eastman

Need a little more spa? Who doesn't? In about an hour, you can be well into the rolling countryside of the Eastern Townships at a lakeside estate set amid forests, meadows, and glades at the foot of Mount Orford. The setting itself will de-stress you from the moment you arrive, if not before; treatments should further the effect, and create restorative memories. Drive out for the day, or stay overnight *(there are 43 rooms)*. Facilities include an indoor and outdoor pool, a steam bath, a meditation room, and exercise equipment. Spa Eastman specializes in rain massage (while being sprinkled by jets of warm water) and watsu (experience shiatsu massage in a pool of hot water), along with aesthetic services.

A day package, starting at $139 without overnight lodging, includes lunch, use of the pool, steam bath, and trails. The Fitness and Wellness Package adds a personal fitness sesssion ($229). Other treatments can include massage, pressotherapy (a detoxifying treatment that stimulates lymph circulation in the legs by means of inflatable boots), and a body wrap, followed by a hydromassage.

For those who can't get away, **Spa Eastman Montreal** offers many of the same services downtown *(666 Rue Sherbrooke Ouest, 16th floor; 514-845-8455; www.spaeastman.com; Métro McGill, green line).*

🛁 Bota-Bota

358 Rue de la Commune Ouest, Old Montreal. 514-284-0333. Open daily 10am–10pm. www.botabota.ca.

This ex-ferry boat is docked at the Old Port, where it offers those seeking rejuventation a unique experience.

Combining originals like a **manicure/pedicure lounge**, **sub-aquatic change rooms**, and a **$200 "passport"** *(good for three months)*, this chic craft has a full menu of treatments as well. Chill out in their wonderful open-air **whirlpool**, after treating yourself to a **Shiatsu**, **Californian**, or **Swedish**

massage, then into their own brand of **Water Circuit** to finish.

Peau Medical/Laser Spa

Seaforth Medical Building, 3550 Chemin de la Côte-des-Neiges, Suite 540, north of Rue Sherbrooke as Rue Guy turns into Chemin de la Côte-des-Neiges. 514-989-7328. Métro Guy, then 165 bus. www.peaumontreal.com

The ultimate esthetique-medical spa offers a complete menu of skin-nourishing techniques, all in a completely "green" suite of rooms, under the direction of world-class dermatologist Dr. Manish Khanna.

SPAS

135

RESTAURANTS

The venues listed below were selected for their ambience, location, and/or value for money. Most restaurants are open daily and accept major credit cards. Call for information regarding reservations, dress code, and opening hours. Restaurants listed are located in Montreal unless otherwise noted. *For a complete listing of restaurants in this guide, see Index.* **Prices** *Rates indicate the average cost of an appetizer, a main course, and a dessert for one person (not including tax, gratuity, or beverages).*

Luxury	**$$$$** More than $75	*Moderate*	**$$** $25 to 50
Expensive	**$$$** $50 to 75	*Inexpensive*	**$** Less than $25

Eating in French

An *entrée* in French is what you have when you begin your dining experience—an "appetizer" or "starter" on the English side of the menu. *Le plat principal* usually goes by the name of "main course" in English. Breakfast, lunch, and dinner in French Canada are *le petit dejeuner, le dîner, and le souper;* no translation is required for *le dessert. Table d'hôte* refers to a fixed-price menu, *often changes daily,* and includes soup/salad, main course, dessert, and sometimes coffee.

MONTREAL

Luxury

La Coupole
$–$$$$ French
1325 Boul. René-Lévèsque Ouest in Hôtel Le Crystal. Daily 6.30am–1am. 514-373-2300. www.restaurantlacoupole.ca
The best deal in the city for an original menu at an affordable price, plus an amazing wine cellar, contemporary design, trained staff, and super location. Try the house risotto, Monaco boullabaisse, famous 30oz rib-steak-for-two, Degustation Menu, or breakfast.

The Beaver Club
$$$$ English
900 Boul. René-Lévesque Ouest, in Fairmont – The Queen Elizabeth Hotel. Closed Sun. 514-861-3511. www.fairmont.com.
Legendary lair of early Montreal's fur-trade tycoons, the Beaver Club maintains a certain tradition. English roast beef, rack of suckling pig, and caribou rosettes are mainstays. Everything is prepared with French savoir-faire—the grilled steak comes with red wine butter, the calf's liver is glazed with sherry vinegar and honey.

Maison Boulud
$$$$ French
1228 Rue Sherbrooke Ouest in the Ritz-Carlton Hotel. 514-842-4212. Open daily. www.ritzmontreal.com
Famed international chef Daniel Boulud creates his magic, after being named honorary chef at Montreal's Highlights Festival. Expect to be impressed by this winner of the James Beard Foundation's "Outstanding Chef." Local ingredients reign and reservations recommended.

Chez Queux

$$$ – $$$$ **French**
158 Rue Saint-Paul Est. 514-866-5194. www.chezqueux.com.
With its massive stone and brick walls, Chez Queux stands out for its reliability, professional service, and comprehensive, award-winning wine list. Classic dishes include Dover sole, or Duck and Wild Berries.

Ferreira Café

$$$ – $$$$ **Portuguese**
1446 Rue Peel. Lunch Mon–Fri 11.45am–3.00pm, dinner from 5.30pm. 514-848-0988. www.ferreiracafe.com.
Carlos Ferreira presents the ambience and cuisine of his country in this Mediterranean-style trattoria. Locals, celebrities, and visiting dignitaries—including the President of Portugal—all flock to sample Portuguese and continental fare such as Gazpacho with Lobster and Coriander, Seafood Cataplana, and Cod with Olive Oil and Tomato Compôte. Racking up some 60,000 bottles, the extensive wine list includes a good selection of white, tawny, and vintage ports.

La Queue de Cheval

$$$$ **American**
1221 Boul. René-Lévesque West. 514-390-0090. Open daily. www.queuedecheval.com.
When is an American-style steak-and-seafood house controversial? When it opens in a city that already has more than its share of fine cuisine establishments. When it's huge and elegant, and demonstrates that American beef, exquisitely prepared, can rival European fare for the attention of the educated palate. Appetizers shine, from an assortment of sausages with mustard to classic steak tartare, and you might even choose an assortment of these over a main course.

M sur Masson

$$ – $$$$ **Classic French Bistro**
2876 Rue Masson Est, Old Rosemont. 514-678-2999. Open daily, Sunday brunch. www.msurmasson.com.
Unpretentious neighborhood bistro serves fresh market dishes with zeal. Try their Lobster Grilled Cheese, Veal Liver (really), or Fish and Chips. Table d'Hôte changes weekly for Sunday brunch. Worth the side-trip into the east-end of the city.

Laloux

$$$ – $$$$ **New French**
250 Ave. des Pins Est. 514-287-9127. www.laloux.com.
Laloux is much sought-after for its surprising nouvelle cuisine, anything from Vegetable Tartare in Gazpacho or Monkfish Pops with Eggplant Caviar to a Burgundian Crêpe with Duck Confit. There is also a fine assortment of wines paired with local cheeses. Large windows and mirrors suggest an establishment on a Parisian boulevard rather than humble surroundings near busy Rue St-Denis.

Narcisse Bistro & Bar à Vin

$$$ – $$$$ **French-Canadian**
93 Rue de la Commune. 514-392-1649. Open daily. www.narcissebistro.com.
Inside the Auberge du Vieux-Port, Narcisse has obvious ties to history while being very much in the contemporary swing of the

city. The food preparation is French-style, adapted to the availability of fresh ingredients. Signature appetizers are Grilled Quail with Honey and Sesame Oil, and Terrine of Braised Duck and Foie Gras; main courses include Venison Seared with Foie Gras, Guinea Hen Supreme, and Suckling Pig. A full traditional Quebec-style dinner will be cooked up for holidays.

Toqué!

$$$$ French

900 Place Jean-Paul-Riopelle, east of Victoria Square. Now open for lunch. Closed Sun & Mon. 514-499-2084. www.restaurant-toque.com.

Toqué! is invariably mentioned among the best and most innovative of Montreal restaurants. The journey from the kitchen of chef Normand Laprise to your plate can involve detours to Japan, the Arctic, or the tropics to yield a complexity of tastes never imagined: Nova Scotia Scallops with Cranberries and Apple Mousse, Tuna Tartare with Sprouts and Jalapeño Cream, Salmon with Citrus, Red Squash and Parmesan Risotto with market vegetables *(for the vegetarian)*. Tasting menus (with or without wine) eliminate the dilemma of what to choose. All served in futuristic premises of glass, steel, and sleek lines.

Moderate

Boris Bistro

$$ French

465 Rue McGill. Open daily. Mon lunch only. 514-848-9575. www.borisbistro.com.

Boris—mascot as well as restaurant—has a loyal following of professionals in Old Montreal, who bring their friends back into the city for dinner. Delightful tavern fare in gleaming surroundings emphasizes le terroir—fine regional products, such as Venison Sausage, Wild Mushroom Fricassée, or Braised Rabbit, when available—along with variations on classics like Duck Confit and Buffalo Steak-Frites. The outdoor patio is a dramatic work of urban archaeology in itself, exposing the frame and stone walls of a building-that-was.

Chez l'Epicier

$$ French

311 St-Paul Est. 514-878-2232. Open daily for dinner 5.30pm– 10pm, lunch Thu/Fri 11.30–2.00pm. www.chezlepicier.com.

This restaurant and wine bar is also, literally, "The Grocer's," with tables set among shelves and in front of counters stocked with delicacies from Quebec and all over. The fare is creative: Parmesan-Oil Ravioli on Duck Confit with Wild Mushrooms, followed by Halibut Marinated in Ginger with a Caviar of Salmon, Mango, and Chives. On a warm day, carry a terrine out to a bench by the Old Port.

Restaurant Bonaparte

$$ French

443 Rue Sainte-Francois-Xavier, Old Montreal. 514-844-4368, inside Auberge Bonaparte. Open daily for breakfast from 6.30am, lunch 11.30am–2pm, dinner from 5.30pm. Theater menu 5.30–6.30pm. www.aubergebonaparte.com.

Entering this location in Old Montreal to dine right next to the Centaur Theatre is something special for numerous reasons. Ownership here almost single-handedly turned the neighborhood around during the lean years, making the ground fertile for more establishments to prosper. Delicious, creative cuisine showcases locally-grown produce, artisan specialties, and a solid wine list. Several different ambiances to dine inside this intimate hallmark of service.

Café Bistro Espace Lafontaine
$$ French
3933 Avenue du Parc-Lafontaine, 514-280-2525. Open Wed–Sun 11am–5pm Labor Day to Jun 24, summertime daily 11am–9pm. espacelafontaine.com,
This once all-but-abandoned City of Montreal restaurant facility, located at the core of a vast park in the Plateau Mont-Royal quarter, has been lovingly renovated and serves fresh market cuisine. Don't think for a moment when you order their "Chien Chaud" that you will receive just any mass-produced hot dog. A sausage handmade on the premises is served in half a fresh baguette, with classic sauerkraut, grilled veggies, and hot mustard on the side. Word on the street says the Steak Tartare is the best in the city and the menu has many options. Good wines, artisanal beer, decadent desserts (try the Key Lime Pie) and Wi-Fi.

Le Petit Moulinsart
$$ Belgian
139 Rue St-Paul Ouest. 514-843-7432. www.lepetitmoulinsart.com.
Step into a corner of Brussels at this little restaurant with its bistro chairs, gleaming light-wood panelling, waiters in bow ties, and pictures paying homage to Tintin, Belgium's most famous comic-character export. The specialty is mussels,

and everything else on the menu is authentic, too, right down to the beers, Belgian fries, Veal à la Rodenbach, and at times Horsemeat Steak Topped with Cheese.

Café Saigon
$$ Chinese
1280 Rue Saint-André, just south of Rue Sainte-Catherine. 514-849-0429. Open daily, Bring-Your-Own wine eatery.
Started by the family matriarch as a Vietnamese sandwich shop next to a Chinese cinema, this gem of the city's eateries offers delicious Imperial rolls, dumplings, Tonkinese soups, Grilled Shrimp and Scallops, General Tao Chicken, and many other inexpensive items. Homemade soy sauce is legendary.

Restaurant Julien
$$ French
1191 Rue Union. 514-871-1581. www.restaurantjulien.com.
Here's an Old Montreal-style restaurant in an uptown setting, with tall glass windows and cozy banquettes. The food style is French, but the flavors come from everywhere, as in Sauteed Vegetables and Tofu Flavored with Cilantro, Sesame-Perfumed Red Tuna Pizza, and Roast Guineafowl Perfumed with Tarragon. The lunchtime *table d'hôte* is good value.

Restaurant du Vieux-Port
$$ Contemporary
39 Rue St-Paul Est. 514-866-3175. www.restaurantduvieuxport.com.
A one-time sailors' inn, the Vieux-Port is a no-pretense, reliable steak and chop house, serving customers in numerous rooms with exposed stone walls. You'll

find Chicken Breast with Shrimp and Garlic Spinach, Filet Mignon with Mushroom Ragoût, and Grilled Salmon, but you won't find a subdued atmosphere. People come here to relax and gab over good food.

Stash Café
$$ Polish
200 Rue Saint-Paul Ouest. 514-845-6611. www.stashcafe.com.
With 30 years at the same Old Montreal location, Stash has outlasted the competition with excellent Polish cuisine. The fare is expectedly hearty: Borscht (beet soup topped with sour cream) to start, *Bigos* (meat-and-sausage stew), Pierogi (dumplings), and Stuffed Cabbage as main courses, with rye bread on the side. For a real Polish feast, enjoy the complete wild boar dinner in season—perfect on a winter's night. The stone surroundings are pure Old Montreal, but you can easily imagine yourself in a castle near the Baltic.

La Tour de Ville
$$ – $$$ International
777 Rue University, at the top of the Delta Centre-Ville Hotel. Open Fri–Sat 5.30pm–11pm, and Sunday brunch 11.30am–3pm. 514-879-4777. www.deltahotels.com.
The name's a play on words (*tour* is turn, tour, and tower) that tells everything: this is Montreal's only revolving restaurant atop the tower of the Delta Centre-Ville Hotel. In the course of the evening you'll enjoy the spectacular sweep of the city—from mountain to skyscrapers to the Montreal Tower and bridges—for at least a spin and a half. It's also a culinary tour, as the cuisine consists of buffets with regional themes—Italian, Japanese, Mediterranean, and more. For somewhat lighter fare with a daytime **view**, try the Sunday brunch. Note: There are only two sittings on Fri or Sat, one from 5.30–8pm, the second from 8–11pm. Reserve ahead.

Bistro Cocagne
$$ – $$$ French
3842 Rue Saint-Denis. Open Sun, Mon & Wed 5.30–10.30pm, Thu–Sat 5.30pm–11.30pm. 514-286-0700. www.bistro-cocagne.com.
Eating in this intimate market-fresh bistro is a joy. From the entrées like Marinated Salmon Marinated in Herbs and Mustard to the heavenly Lamb Ravioli served with Mushrooms, Caramelized Onions, and White Truffle oil, the plates build to a crescendo of taste delights, with regulars like Roast Duck, Rabbit Leg, or Macaronade with Sauce Foie-Gras, which simply make you want more.

Inexpensive

Café des Lettres/Presse Café
$ International
475 Boul. de Maisonneuve Est, inside the Grande Bibliothéque (main library). 514-499-2999. Presse Café open library hours Tue–Sun 10am–10pm, Café des Lettres open Tue–Fri for lunch 11am–3pm.
The city's best-kept dining secret, many locals don't even know about. Library users enter the main entrance, but near the side entrance, you'll discover a delicious option for lunch in Café des Lettres, or a super lunch counter in Presse Café. The same kitchen serves market-fresh fare to both. Specials, fresh pasta, pizza, soups, and desserts.

L'Académie

$ – $$ Italian
4051 Rue Saint-Denis. 514-849-2249. www.lacademie.ca. Métro Sherbrooke.

At L'Académie, gleaming chrome, spare lines, and floor-to-ceiling glass suggest a contemporary Roman bistro. Gnocchi with Gorgonzola Sauce and Veal Scallops in Mustard Sauce, along with low prices, attract customers who line up, bottle of wine in hand. The *table d'hôte* specialty of the day includes dishes such as Swordfish with Avocado Salsa.

Tataki

$ – $$ Japanese
61 Rue Duluth. 514-842-5580. Open Mon–Fri 11am–10pm, Sat–Sun 2pm–10pm.

When you are in the Plateau Mont-Royal and must have sushi, this tiny counter, grocery, and sit-down appeals to all sushi tastes, especially the pocketbook. Where else can you get lunch starting at $5.95 and walk away feeling satisfied? Take a party platter back to your hotel for as little as $10.95, and purchase grocery items such as teas, spices, noodles, and Japanese pop drinks.

Magnan

$ – $$ Steakhouse
2602 Rue Saint-Patrick. 514-935-9647. www.magnanresto.com.

This cavernous tavern south of the Atwater Market, across from the Lachine Canal, speaks in working-class tones, with plywood paneling, photos of local celebrities, and hearty fare. And the patrons speak both languages, switching effortlessly from unaccented English to unaccented French. A patented roast beef and steaks

are mainstays, and depending on the season, you might also find mussels, salmon, or surprisingly low-priced lobster. The beer is cheap, and much of it consumed upstairs while watching hockey and football on television.

Le Taj

$ – $$ Indian
2077 Rue Stanley. 514-845-9015. www.restaurantletaj.com.

The decor may be generic, but the food is genuine Northern Indian and attracts a following of businessmen, professors, and politicians who know good value. The specialty is marinated meats cooked in a tandoor (a traditional clay oven), and there's a good assortment of curries. Plates of fresh, hot *naan* bread go perfectly with excellent mulligatawny soup. The lunchtime buffet is excellent value – all items are from the menu, with no starchy or fried fillers.

Basha

$ Lebanese
930 Rue Sainte-Catherine Ouest, upstairs. 514-866-4272.

This Lebanese fast-food firm has numerous outlets around central Montreal, in and out of the Underground City and mini-malls. At this location, you get an excellent choice of kebabs, salads, and vegetarian spreads, such as hummus served with pita, for very little outlay—plus a ringside seat to watch all the goings-on on busy Rue Sainte-Catherine below.

Passé Composé

$ French/American
950 Rue Roy, corner Mentana, Métro Sherbrooke. Open Wed–Sun 8.30am –2.30pm, Fri–Sat for dinner from

6pm.passecomposerestaurant.com
For a breakfast like the locals enjoy, try this neighborhood haunt near Parc La Fontaine. Always a comfort zone inside this intimate eatery, with super breakfast platters, lunch specials, inventive dinners, strong coffee, and a good floor show near the Gay Village.

La Maison des Pâtes Fraîches
$ Italian
865 Rue Rachel Est, just east of Rue Saint-Hubert. 514-527-5487. www.lamaisonpatesfraiches.com.
For a stellar Italian homecooked menu of pastas, pizza, daily specials, sauces, sandwiches, gelato, and the best cappuccino in the city (at the best price too!), this is where locals come in droves. A bank of freezers supplies frozen goodies to take home (lasagna, tortellini, etc.), and there's even fresh vegetables, breads, parmesan by the pound, and *cannoli* you should not miss. The music is great, the floor show non-stop, and the front corner table best for watching the Plateau Mont-Royal passers-by.

Luca E Franco
$ – $$ Italian
3443 Rue Saint-Denis, just above Rue Sherbrooke. 514-507-9700.
Following a long apprenticeship at his mother's *La Maison des Pâtes Fraîches* (above), son Roberto's new "osteria" welcomes diners to a chic contemporary setting, featuring a tapas menu, wood-oven pizzas, and a dynamite perch to watch the action along popular Rue Saint-Denis. Try catch of the day, and it's a great place for Happy Hour.

Rotisserie Panama
$ – $$ Greek
789 Rue Jean-Talon Est, west of Avenue Parc. 514-276-5223. Open daily 11am–11pm. www.rotisseriepanama.com.
Montreal story: Two Greek guys go to Panama and open two eateries and do really well. They come back to Montreal and open two more *(2nd location at Marché-Ouest).* When the urge for a great Greek meal hits you, Panama is the place to satisfy all your senses AND your pocketbook. Famous for their roasted meats, everything on the menu is simply great.

Le Commensal
$ – $$ Vegetarian
1204 Ave. McGill College. 514-871-1480. 1720 Rue St-Denis, 514-845-2627.
Cafeteria set-up, the Commensal chain serves vegetarian *haute cuisine* to rival the fare in more conventional restaurants. Choose

---

Joining In
You haven't truly experienced the Latin Quarter until you've lingered over an *apéro* (aperitif) or an espresso, while fellow patrons hunch over school texts or debate the *question of the day*. Favorite places for a beverage are **Presse Café** *(1750 Rue St-Denis)*, the **Café des Lettres** in the **Grande Bibliothéque** *(475 Rue de Maisonneuve Est)*, or vegetarian **Le Commensal** *(1720 Rue St-Denis)*. Farther north, you can slyly gauge the hottest restaurants by the length of the line on Saturday night. **L'Académie** *(4051 Rue St-Denis at Duluth; 514-849-2249)*, with its low prices and Italian menu, rates high by this standard.

your courses and pay by weight. Terrines, lasagnas, and vegetable chilis have a wide following, and are also available in supermarkets.

Chalet BBQ
$ – $$ American
5456 Rue Sherbrooke Ouest, Exit 64 off Decarie Expressway. 514-489-7235. www.chaletbbq.com.
Since 1944, this rustic venue has made legions of friends with its patented chicken, sauce, and price. Kings and queens, beggars, and hockey players all come here because of the consistent product. Home delivery services a huge area, even downtown hotels.

Restaurant La Paryse
$ – $$ American
302 Rue Ontario Est, corner Rue Sanguinet, Quartier-Latin. 514-842-2040. Closed Sun & Mon. Open 11am–11pm.
The burgers here are considered the best in the city. Paryse's place is tiny, though so don't be surprised to see a lineup at any time of the year. Double and veggie burgers, as well as super club sandwiches, deliriously good fries, wines by the glass, beer, and great sweets and coffees. A winner since 1980.

Schwartz's Hebrew Deli
$ Delicatessen
3895 Boul. Saint-Laurent. 514-842-4813. www.schwartzsdeli.com. Métro Saint-Laurent. Open 8am–12.30am Sun–Thu, 8am–1.30am Fri, 8am–2.30am Sat.
Jewish-style cuisine is not the same everywhere. Montreal's specialty is smoked meat, with flavor achieved by secret spices and the characteristic smoke of local hardwoods. It's served piled

on rye bread, and nowhere so generously. *(New take-out venue next door.)*

Mamie Clafoutis
$ – $$ International
1291 Avenue Van Horne (Métro Outremont), or 3600 Rue Saint-Denis (Métro Sherbrooke). 514-750-7245. www.mamieclafoutis.com.
The hallmark of these two shops is the quality of the goods prepared onsite for clients who demand the best breads, cakes, clafoutis, sandwiches, quiches, pies, and salads. Agree not to speak about calories when you enter, and just enjoy the heavenly products, then go for a nice long walk.

Première Moisson
$ French
Atwater Market, Métro Lionel Groulx. 514-932-0328. www.premieremoisson.com.
This chain of bakery/pastry shops has many outlets, but the most enticing is the location on the upper level of Atwater Market, where there's ample terrace-style seating in all seasons. Fill up on pastries, quiches, chocolatines, and sausages, or just linger over a cup of coffee. Afterward, wander past the nearby vendors' stalls and sample cheeses, patés, terrines, and spices from around the world.

Café Santropol
$ Canadian
3990 Rue Saint-Urbain. 514-842-3110. Métro Saint-Laurent and bus 55 to Rue Duluth, then walk west. www.santropol.com.
The dream has never faded at Café Santropol, a sixties alternative cafe now in gracious middle age. The hammered-tin ceiling was

antique when the place began, and everything is just a bit more worn and comfortable with each new year. Enjoy tall cheese, fruit and nut sandwiches on brown bread, along with thick soups and fruit shakes. Part of what you pay goes to support a meals-on-wheels program.

QUEBEC CITY

Luxury

L'Astral
$$$ – $$$$ French
Inside Hotel Loews Le Concorde, 1225 Cours du General-de-Montcalm. 418-780-3602. www.lastral.ca.
If there's a city made for viewing from a variety of vantage points, it's Quebec. L'Astral offers a great **viewpoint**, in a revolving restaurant atop Hôtel Le Concorde. The byways of the Old City and the valley of the St. Lawrence spread before you in an ever-changing **panorama**. All this comes with fine French cooking, such as Filet Mignon in an Aubergine Crust. Watching the pennies? Go for the lunch buffet or the early dinner.

Laurie Raphaël
$$$ – $$$$ French
117 Rue Dalhousie. 418-692-4555, or in Montreal at 2050 Rue Mansfield. 514-985-6072. www.laurieraphael.com.
On the outside, Laurie Raphaël is a contemporary glass pavilion attached to a modern building, but inside, it's Quebec City's premier adventurous gourmet establishment, a world music of cuisine with a solid French base. Chef Daniel Vézina's changing

menu features artisanal Quebecois products such as smoked salmon and emu from the Charlevoix region.

Restaurant L'Échaudé
$$$ – $$$$ French
73 Rue Sault-au-Matelot. 418-692-1299. www.echaude.com.
Plates are served as they would be in Paris, in a setting fitted with light-colored wainscoting and decorated generously with plants. Inventive takes on classics include Medallions of Venison with Wild Berry Sauce, Duck Confit, and Grilled Steak with a Mango Sauce. A lunch menu and inclusive dinner menu are available.

Le Saint-Amour
$$$ – $$$$ French
48 Rue Sainte-Ursule. 418-694-0667. www.saint-amour.com.
For a quarter-century, chef Jean-Luc Boulay has been leading the way in merging regional ingredients from Quebec with the classic cooking methods of France. Caribou Steak with Juniper Berries, Foie Gras of Quebec Duck Prepared Six Ways, or Salmon Tartare and Snow Crab with Avocado Mousse may appear on the menu, along with Filet Mignon or lobster. Your choice of dining areas includes the **Winter Garden**, a high-ceilinged, Victorian conservatory.

Moderate

Café du Monde
$$ French
84 Rue Dalhousie. 418-692-4455. www.lecafedumonde.com.
The premier locale for river gazing in all seasons is upstairs in the modern cruise terminal, where

Café du Monde fuses bistro decor with huge expanses of glass. The food smacks of French bistro fare with a local take: Black Pudding and Duck Confit are mainstays, along with Venison Brochette with Berries, all of which goes down well on a frosty day.

Portofino
$$ **Italian**
54 Rue Couillard. 418-692-8888. www.portofino.qc.ca.
For informal and reliable dining on familiar and well-prepared Italian specialties, Portofino is there, with pizzas cooked in a wood-burning oven—a Quebec specialty—an assortments of pasta, as well as classic veal dishes. Prices are reasonable, the atmosphere is relaxed, and you can watch the food being prepared in the open kitchen. Live musicians, too.

Voo-Doo Grill
$$ **Asian**
575 Grande Allée. 418-647-2000. www.voodoogrill.com.
It's all about the food *and* style *and* presentation at the Voo-Doo Grill. Dark hardwood fittings, tropical plants, and oversize statuary create the air of an eccentric's mansion somewhere in Southeast Asia. Tandoori Shrimp, Grain-Fed Citrus Chicken with "Volcano" Sauce, and Grilled Wild Salmon with Lobster Sauce are house mainstays. *Cigar lounge.*

Table
$$ **International**
395 Rue de la Couronne, inside the Hotel PUR. www.hotelpur.com.
Design fans will love the effort invested here, as sleek meets functional, wood meets steel, and the food matches the promise of the hotel's contemporary chic. Fresh local ingredients handled with love are the compelling reason to visit this Saint-Roch eatery.

Inexpensive

L'Ardoise
$ **Belgian**
71 Rue Saint-Paul. 418-694-0213.
The wood paneling and cafe chairs at L'Ardoise in the Lower Town are a slice of Brussels, and so are the *moules-frites* (mussels and fries). Select your favorite dipping sauces and dive right in. Brunch menu available as well on weekends.

Le Cochon Dingue
$ – $$ **French-Canadian**
46 Boul. Champlain. 418-692-2013. www.cochondingue.com.
In Lower Town, where formal eateries flourish, the Cochon Dingue ("Crazy Pig") is anything but stuffy. Locals come here to feast on breakfast panini, classic steak-*frites*, *poutine* (a Quebecois specialty: French fries topped with cheese curds and brown gravy), and deep-dish pies and *tourtes*. Kids get their own menu, too. Several other locations also, so check website or call.

Casse-Crêpe Breton
$ **French**
1136 Rue Saint-Jean. 418-692-0438. cassecrepebreton.com.
No American pancake house was ever this good. Classic, impossibly thin crêpes of Brittany are served with dozens of fillings, from apple compôte to hearty sausage. Don't forget to ask for maple syrup.

RESTAURANTS

HOTELS

The properties listed below were selected for their ambience, location, and/or value for money. Prices reflect the average cost for a standard double room for two people *(not including applicable taxes)*. Hotels in Montreal often offer special discount packages. Properties are located in Montreal, unless otherwise specified. For a complete list of hotels mentioned in this guide, see Index.

Prices and Amenities *Price ranges do not include the Canadian hotel tax, or the sales tax of 14%.*

Luxury	**$$$$** More than $350	*Moderate*	**$$** $175 to 250
Expensive	**$$$** $250 to 350	*Inexpensive*	**$** $100 to 175

Luxury

⛤ Hôtel Le Crystal
$$$ – $$$$ **131 suites**
1100 Rue de la Montagne.
514-861-5550 or 877-861-5550.
www.hotellecrystal.com.
Located at the corner of Boul. René-Lévesque West, kitty-korner to the **Centre Bell** hockey forum, this sculptured glass creation has literally changed the landscape of the neighborhood. The clientele is a show by themselves, so don't be surprised to see world-famous hockey players, F1 racing drivers, or film stars staying here.
It helps to have the incomparable **La Coupole Restaurant** onsite, plus **IZBA** spa, and a stellar concierge team.

Hôtel Le Germain
$$$$ **101 rooms**
2050 Rue Mansfield.
514-849-2050 or 877-333-2050.
www.germainmontreal.com.
This office building/boutique hotel oozes refined luxury. Oriental minimalism prevails in the light-filled loft-like rooms, done in earth tones with dark wood furnishings handcrafted by local artisans. Sumptuous bedding and upscale amenities such as irons and ironing boards, CD players, and daily newspapers make these some of the most sought-after rooms in the city.

⛤ Hôtel Le Saint-James
$$$$ **61 rooms**
355 Rue Saint-Jacques Ouest.
514-841-3111 or 866-841-3111.
www.hotellestjames.com.
The grandest of the boutique hotels of Montreal, the Saint-James has re-vivified the tiered Beaux-Arts Merchant Bank Building. The sumptuous two-story grand salon, elegant spaces, secluded nooks, and the exciting **XO Le Restaurant** and **XO Le Lounge** seamlessly weave the former stuffy banking hall into the 21C. Rooms are mansion-like, rather than hotel-style, with hardwood paneling, paintings, brocades, custom carpets, artwork, and marble-lined bathrooms.
High tea is served in the afternoon, and the library is as much a haven as a private club. The St-James is conveniently located beside the Montreal World Trade Centre, Underground City, and Palais du Congrés convention center. Member of **Leading Hotels of the World**.

MUST STAY

Loews Hotel Vogue

$$$$ **142 rooms**
1425 Rue de la Montagne.
514-285-5555 or 866-768-6658.
www.loewshotels.com.
The Vogue is plain on the outside,
as if to disguise its sumptuous
interior ornamentation. While
rooms are small, they are elegantly
decorated with heavy curtains, silk
upholstery, and French Provincial
lamps, and have every amenity—
right down to the marble-tiled
bathroom with whirlpool tub.
The Vogue sits near the **Museum
of Fine Arts** and the shops along
Rue Sainte-Catherine and **Rue
Sherbrooke**. Babysitting, pet care,
and laundry service onsite. *Ask for
the Local Flavors menu.*

Auberge du Vieux-Port

$$$ – $$$$ **27 rooms**
97 Rue de la Commune Est.
514-876-0081 or 888-612-3917.
www.aubergeduvieuxport.com.
A one-time riverfront warehouse
and general store serves as
an ultra-charming setting for
comfortable rooms, more relaxed
in tone than in other Old Montreal
boutique hotels. In the guest
rooms, reproduction 18C brass
bedsteads and chairs are set
against exposed brick and stone
walls, and sun streams in through
huge windows that afford **views** of
the St. Lawrence River on the south
side. The **rooftop terrace/bar** has
the best hotel perch over the Old
Port of all the competition.
*Larger loft-style accommodations
are also available; all room rates
includes breakfast and afternoon
wine and snacks.*
Rainspa is located steps away, and
onsite French bistro fare awaits at
Narcisse eatery/winebar.

Fairmont The Queen Elizabeth

$$$$ **1,037 rooms**
900 Boul. René-Lévesque Ouest.
514-861-3511 or 800-441-1414.
www.fairmont.com.
Queen of Montreal hotels is a
bastion of tradition, style, and taste,
and also sits atop the city's Gare-
Centrale train station. The fabled
Beaver Club ($$$) continues to lead
the city's culinary offerings; the
lobby **Tea Lounge ($)** serves classic
afternoon English tea and informal
Montréalais ($$) is a travelers' hub,
serving mediterranean cuisine
and super **Sunday brunch**. With
high-speed Internet access and
a separate breakfast area, the
Gold Level has its own access via
a **panoramic elevator** running
up the outside of the building.
Gibson Spa *(514-866-6639)* is the
oldest in Canada, and no wonder.
Personalized service leads here.

Hostellerie Pierre du Calvet

$$$$ **9 rooms**
405 Rue Bonsecours. 514-282-
1725 or 866-544-1725.
www.pierreducalvet.ca.
This historic house *(see Landmarks)*
has all the makings of a memorable
stay, in rooms with fireplaces and
beamed ceilings, furnished with
massive antiques and canopy beds.
Uneven floors and exposed stone
walls are not re-creations, but the
real thing. Noted for its French
cuisine and Quebec ingredients, the
Pierre du Calvet ($$$) restaurant
serves such dishes as Venison
Paupiettes and Filet Mignon in its
dramatic, high-ceilinged space.
A lighter lunch menu is available
in the adjacent **Les Filles du Roy**
($–$$). Covered greenhouse patio
is pleasant for breakfast, even
in winter.

HOTELS

Hôtel Gault

$$$$ **29 rooms**

449 Rue Sainte-Hélène.
514-904-1616 or 866-904-1616.
www.hotelgault.com.
At the Gault, minimalist modern
design takes center-stage against
the background of an 1871 cotton
importer's warehouse. Outside,
the premises are ornate, inspired
by the Beaux-Arts buildings of
contemporary Paris. Inside, only the
original cast-iron stanchions remain,
contrasting with unornamented
steel, concrete, and white oak. Loft-
like guest rooms are large and open,
and decked out with contemporary
designer furnishings. Consistent
with partial ownership by media
mogul Daniel Langlois, state-of-the-
art entertainment consoles enhance
each room. Rue Sainte-Hélène is
one of the quietest streets in
Old Montreal.

Hotel InterContinental Montréal

$$$$ **357 rooms**

360 Rue St-Antoine Ouest.
514-987-9900 or 800-361-3600.
montreal.intercontinental.com.
Although its turrets and roof
may resemble a castle, the
InterContinental offers intimate
spaces. It's even possible to
overlook the lobby and check-in
area if you're not familiar with the
property, tucked behind a row of
historic facades in the Montreal
World Trade Centre. Carpets,
upholstered chairs, and fluffy
linens are straight out of Paris. This
is as close as you'll come to Old
Montreal and still be in a large,
full-service hotel, with a health
club, convention facilities, and an
all-season rooftop lap pool. **OSCO**
(**$$$**) serves local ingredients in

Provence style, while **Chez Plume**
(**$$**) in the Nordheimer annexe has
a relaxed British pub ambiance.

Hotel W Montréal

$$$$ **152 rooms**

901 Square-Victoria. 514-395-
3100 or 888-627-7081.
www.whotels.com/montreal.
Sleek W style goes perfectly with
Montreal, from the spaceship
lines of the Wunderbar to Zen-like
room and bath fittings, to the cozy
goose-down comforters, electronic
amenities, and on-site spa. The
financial center and Underground
City are just steps away. Dine at
Ristorante Otto (**$$$**) to experience
a fusion of Mediterranean and
exotic flavors with characteristic
Quebec fresh market ingredients.

Hôtel Le Saint-Sulpice

$$$$ **108 rooms**

414 Rue Saint-Sulpice. 514-288-
1000 or 877-785-7423.
www.lesaintsulpice.com.
Although it was built to the scale
and profile of Old Montreal, the
Saint-Sulpice is a recent hotel.
Rooms and public areas off the
garden courtyard are flooded with
natural light, and generous use of
dark hardwoods and leather make
for an environment that's modern
but still warm. Guest rooms are
large suites, either with open-plan
or separate bedroom; all have a
microwave, many with fireplaces,
and all have high-speed Internet
connections. Try **S Restaurant** (**$$$**)
and **summertime garden**.

Hôtel Nelligan

$$$$ **105 rooms**

106 Rue Saint-Paul Ouest.
514-788-2040 or 877-788-2040.
www.hotelnelligan.com.

"Nelligan" is of Irish origin, to be sure, but in Quebec, the name refers to Émile Nelligan—poet, romantic, bon-vivant, exemplar of good taste—all the qualities epitomized in this boutique hotel. Set in a 19C building, stone and brick walls establish the period atmosphere, along with dark wood furnishings and plush chairs. A former courtyard with a greenhouse roof, the atrium is bordered by grillwork and decorated with plants. Public spaces, including a library, are cozy and conducive to conversation. **Verses Restaurant ($$$)** makes an elegant setting for local specialties.

Hôtel Omni Mont-Royal
$$$ – $$$$ 299 rooms
1050 Rue Sherbrooke Ouest.
514-284-1110 or 800-843-6664.
www.omnihotels.com.
A solid and respected doyenne, the Omni has maintained its quality and standards through several changes of identity *(formerly Westin, formerly Four Seasons)*. You won't find idiosyncrasies or nooks and crannies, but rather solid and reliable service, stately public areas with clean lines paneled in light marble, and amenities that include in-room Internet access and CD players. A rare treat is the **heated outdoor pool**, which is open all year. The location is convenient to McGill University and the central shopping area.

Place d'Armes Hôtel & Suites
$$$$ 133 rooms
55 Rue Saint-Jacques Ouest.
514-842-1887 or 888-450-1887.
www.hotelplacedarmes.com.
Following current trends in boutique hotels, the Place d'Armes is not a restoration, but an impressive re-use of the dramatic spaces of the former Great Scottish Life Insurance Building and adjacent structures. Beaux-Arts architectural detailing serves as a background to updated Art-Deco and contemporary furnishings and elements. With their exposed brick walls, rooms are at once homey and state-of-the-art, with Internet connections and large bathrooms. The rooftop terrace/bar **Terrace Place d'Armes** offers wonderful **views** down to Place d'Armes and Old Montreal. **Rainspa** has Montreal's only *hammam* (Oriental steam bath).

Hotel St. Paul
$$$$ 120 rooms
355 Rue McGill. 514-380-2222 or 866 -380-2202. www.hotelstpaul.com.
A landmark in Montreal's business district for more than a century, the Canadian Express Building is now a showcase of Modernist design, from the stunning, illuminated-from-inside alabaster lobby fireplace to rooms with white leather sofas, suspended light fixtures, and gleaming black floors. **Vauvert Restaurant ($$$)** is an adventure in dining each time you try it. Imagination reigns and anything is possible, so bring your sense of curiosity and know there is no mass cooking going on here. Try the cold foie-gras, the filet mignon, and the cheeseake.

Hyatt Regency Montréal
$$$$ 605 rooms
1255 Rue Jeanne-Mance.
514-982-1234 or 800-361-8234.
www.montreal.hyatt.com.
In itself, the Hyatt Regency is a fine hotel, with numerous services

and dining choices, convention facilities, indoor pool, gym, and sundeck. But what sets it apart is its integration into the **Place Desjardins commercial and office complex**. Descend by elevator into the adjacent grand space for boutique browsing or festival events, and continue without stepping outside to Place des Arts, the Métro, and the Palais-des-Congrès convention center. Many rooms provide premier viewing for summer's **Jazz Fest** and winter's **Montreal High Lights Festival**; in the hallways and restaurant you may spy the festival stars themselves.

The Ritz-Carlton Montreal
$$$$ 130 rooms
1228 Rue Sherbrooke Ouest.
514-842-4212 or 800-363-0366.
www.ritzmontreal.com.
For generations, the rich and powerful who have visited Montreal have stayed in this grande dame, while the local rich and powerful have held court in the public spaces. Recently updated and impeccably maintained, the Ritz envelops its clientele in plush upholstered furniture, chandeliers and mirrors in the classic French hotel style. Full appreciation requires dinner in the **Maison Boulud ($$$)** featuring 3-star Michelin chef **Daniel Boulud**.

Sofitel Montréal Golden Mile
$$$ – $$$$ 258 rooms
1155 Rue Sherbrooke Ouest.
514-285-9000 or 866-332-3590.
www.sofitel.com.
From bright Provençal colors to serene marble bathrooms, to the lobby with its wall-of-light reception desk, the entire

experience here is pleasing and soothing for the well-heeled business traveler at the Sofitel. No-pretense Art Moderne styling and excellent service will also attract those seeking a hotel not usually found on this continent. Amenities include a **fitness center** and **sauna**, and **high-speed Internet access**, but no pool. Gourmet dining at award-winning **Renoir** onsite.

Hilton Montréal Bonaventure
$$$$ 395 rooms
900 de La Gauchetière Ouest.
514-878-2332 or 800-267-2575.
www.hiltonmontreal.com.
Anonymously set atop the Place Bonaventure shopping complex and exhibition halls, the downtown Hilton pleasantly surrounds a **rooftop garden courtyard** and **four-season outdoor pool**. Its **Le Castillon Restaurant ($$$)** is a re-creation of the great hall of a château with a reasonably priced lunchtime buffet. Underground City provides sheltered access to the convention center, foodcourt, and **VIA Rail** trains.

Moderate

Auberge Bonaparte
$$ 31 rooms
447 Rue St-François-Xavier. 514-844-1448. www.bonaparte.com.
Here's a rare Old Montreal hotel that looks as if it's been functioning for years—in the best sense. Its attractive furnishings suggest the era of Napoleon, and its **restaurant ($$)** serves good French cuisine behind a glass storefront. Add to this a *salon* with fireplace, and rates that include breakfast and Internet connections in rooms individually decorated with

wardrobes and large windows, and you've got a recipe for success.

Auberge Bonsecours
$$ 7 rooms
353 Rue St-Paul Est. 514-396-2662.
www.aubergebonsecours.com.
Auberge Bonsecours carves cheery rooms in warm Provence yellows and reds out of a small former warehouse set at the back of a renovated historic stable yard. Exposed brick and stone, sloping attic ceilings, and unexpected twists and corners add to the idiosyncratic charm of this inn, all nicely finished and maintained *(and well air-conditioned in summer)*. Room rates for singles are quite a bit lower than the price for doubles, but either way, the price includes a buffet breakfast.

Auberge de la Fontaine
$$ 21 rooms
1301 Rue Rachel Est.
514-597-0166 or 800-597-0597.
www.aubergedelafontaine.com.
This urban inn has charms, with cheerful rooms individually decorated, some with balconies and exposed brick walls. The location is opposite La Fontaine Park, yet it's not far from **Rue Saint-Denis** and some of the most edgy shops and restaurants. Room rates include breakfast and parking.

Auberge les Passants du Sans Soucy
$$ 9 rooms
171 Rue St-Paul Ouest. 514-842-2634. www.lesanssoucy.com.
The intimate Sans Soucy pioneered the revival of Old Montreal as a lodging area for visitors with refined tastes. The inn carries on its reputation with exquisite

furnishings and careful attention to detail in its nine rooms, each boasting a beamed ceiling, wood floor, iron or massive wood beds, exposed stone walls, and fireplaces—not to mention modern baths, Internet connections and air conditioning.
There's even an **art gallery** showcasing talent from the province. *Breakfast is included. Reserve early.*

Château Versailles
$$ 65 rooms
1659 Rue Sherbrooke Ouest.
514-933-3611 or 888-933-8111.
chateauversaillesmontreal.com.
Fashioned from a row of elegant Golden Square Mile town houses, the Château Versailles is much the English manor hotel in Montreal. Salons and some rooms have wainscoting, elaborate fireplaces, moldings, and chandeliers. Ground-floor rooms are decorated in cheerful colors but lack the period touches.
The château lies at the beginning of a residential area, less noisy than elsewhere downtown, and only a couple of blocks from the Museum of Fine Arts and Rue Sainte-Catherine.

Holiday Inn Select
$$ 235 rooms
99 Ave. Viger Ouest.
514-878-9888 or 888-878-9888.
www.yul-downtown.hiselect.com.
The house doctor is an acupuncturist, the gift shop sells lacquerware and vases, and the hotel's **Chez Chine ($$)** restaurant includes a pagoda and a huge coy pond filled with colorful fish. Altogether, you might forget that you're in Montreal. In fact, you're

right in Chinatown, just steps from Old Montreal, the convention center, and Boul. Saint-Laurent.

Hôtel de la Montagne
$$ **142 rooms**
1430 Rue de la Montagne.
514-288-5656 or 800-361-6262.
www.hoteldelamontagne.com.
Hôtel de la Montagne is in the midst of the central downtown restaurant and bar scene. It connects to **Les Beaux Jeudis (Thursday's) Restaurant ($$)** on Rue Crescent and is consciously trendy, starting with the doorman in top hat. The hotel's more than show, however, with comfortable traditional furnishings in English or French country themes, and amenities that include a **rooftop pool**.

Hôtel de l'Institut
$$ **42 rooms**
3535 Rue Saint-Denis.
514-282-5120 or 800-361-5111.
www.ithq.qc.ca/hotel.
L'Institut is the hotel trade's counterpart to a teaching hospital. You'll get eager service from staffers who are learning the business, overseen by pros with years of experience. Completely renovated, the location along lively Rue Saint-Denis near the Latin Quarter couldn't be more of a tonic, overlooking **Carré Saint-Louis** park and fountain.

Lhotel
$$ **61 rooms**
262 Rue Saint-Jacques Ouest.
514-985-0019 or 877-553-0019.
www.lhotelmontreal.com.
The "Nineteenth Century" Hotel combines attributes of Old

Montreal's newer boutique hotels—a stately older bank building, ample grand spaces, softened formality, and period charm—with more reasonable rates than elsewhere on this street. Decorative updates in public areas are black-and-white, in subdued Art-Deco style, while rooms are done across a wide swathe of styles, from mid-19C French decor, to sedate, to modern. Valet service is prized.

Sheraton Montréal Aéroport
$$ **482 rooms**
12505 Côte-de-Liesse, Dorval.
514-631-2411 or 800-567-2411.
sheratonmontrealairport.com.
Just minutes from the new terminal by free 24-hour shuttle, this huge, completely renovated airport hotel has been a long time coming. With sleekly-styled rooms, **solarium health club**, and dining options in line with contemporary needs, the **landscaped grounds**, **outdoor pool**, and **long-term parking** add to the appeal. *Express buses and VIA Rail commuter trains provide one-stop access to downtown.*

SpringHill Suites
$$ **124 rooms**
445 Rue Saint-Jean-Baptiste.
514-875-4333 or 866-875-4333.
www.springhillsuites.com.
The low-rise building of the Marriott SpringHill Suites hardly intrudes on Old Montreal. Inside, it's all modern and low-key, with predictable comforts including an indoor pool and garage, and a microwave and a refrigerator in the rooms. The new connects with the old: a passage leads to **Auberge St-Gabriel ($$$)**,

one of the old city's more venerable restaurants, offering French and Quebec fare, and just around the corner on Rue Notre-Dame is **CAMTEC** for your photo needs.

Inexpensive

Angelica Blue Bed and Breakfast

$ **5 rooms**
1213 Rue Sainte-Elisabeth.
514-288-5969.
www.angelicablue.com.
The residential block of brick houses and wooden porches off busy Boulevard René-Lévesque is a surprise, and so too is this guesthouse, with its friendly management and sunny, high-ceilinged rooms outfitted with down comforters, robes, and hairdryers. You'll have to walk a couple of blocks to anywhere, but "anywhere" includes Rue Saint-Denis, Place des Arts, the heart of Montreal's festival neighborhood, and the all-alluring Old Port. *Breakfast is included.*

Anne ma soeur Anne Hôtel-Studio

$ **32 rooms**
4119 Rue Saint-Denis.
514-281-3187 or 877-281-3187.
www.annemasoeuranne.com.
"Anne-my-sister-Anne" has more going for it than a mouthful of a name and virtual exclusivity as a lodging place in the trendy **Plateau Mont-Royal** area. Contemporary-style rooms have all been re-done, many with Murphy beds, and all with microwave and refrigerator, plus high-speed Internet connection. *The rate includes breakfast.* There are stairs to climb.

Auberge Le Jardin d'Antoine

$ **25 rooms**
2024 Rue Saint-Denis.
514-843-4506 or 800-361-4506.
www.aubergelejardindantoine.com.
This nicely renovated town house expresses the gentility of bygone days, with polished woodwork and floral wallpaper and bedspreads. It's tranquil inside, despite the active street scene, and the rate includes a continental breakfast. Artisan shopping abounds here.

Hôtel Saint-Denis

$ **50 rooms**
1254 Rue Saint-Denis.
514-849-4526 or 800-363-3364.
www.hotel-st-denis.com.
Now into its tenth decade, the Saint-Denis has been renovated with care, while not putting on airs. Comfortable and well-lit rooms are decorated with pieces that might have come from the local furniture store. And it's a safe haven in the **Latin Quarter**, where not all accommodations rent by the night.

Manoir Ambrose

$ **22 rooms**
3422 Rue Stanley.
514-288-6922 or 888-688-6922.
www.manoirambrose.com.
Can't afford to stay in the ritziest area of town? Think again. It's not the Ritz, but Manoir Ambrose, a series of connected town houses that provides odd-shaped rooms, with old-style furnishings and personalized service just steps away from the **Museum of Fine Arts**. *Continental breakfast is included in the rate.*

HOTELS

Hotel Quartier-Latin Montréal

$ **39 rooms**

1763 Rue St-Denis.
514-842-8444 or 866-843-8444.
www.hotel-quartierlatin.com.
For bare-bones budget basic,
you'll get more than you pay for
at this hotel. Renovated modern
rooms have private baths and a
continental breakfast is included
each morning. The lively Latin
Quarter location is also included.

Castel Saint-Denis Hôtel

$ **18 rooms**

2099 Rue St-Denis. 514-842-9719.
www.castelsaintdenis.qc.ca.
Here's an unpretentious hotel
with just a few touches of style,
such as wainscoted walls. It's
clean and centrally air-conditioned,
and rates as a "must" in the low-
budget category.

QUEBEC CITY

Luxury

Auberge Saint-Antoine

$$$$ **95 rooms**

8 Rue St-Antoine.
418-692-2211 or 888-692-2211.
www.saint-antoine.com.
Part of the upscale **Relais &
Chateaux** chain, the Saint-Antoine
wraps 21C luxury inside an 18C
warehouse in **Lower Town**. Rooms
in both the structures boast
exposed brick walls, comfortable
modern styling, and down duvets
and pillows. Large windows that
open, free high-speed Internet
access, and heated bathroom
floors add thoughtful touches.
Throughout the inn, the city's
history lives on in the form of 18C
artifacts displayed in glassed-in wall
cases. Be sure to make reservations

for a meal at **Panache** restaurant
(**$$$**). Specializing in contemporary
Canadian cuisine, Panache fills
the charming space in the former
warehouse's storage area.

Fairmont Le Château Frontenac

$$$$ **618 rooms**

1 Rue des Carrières.
418-692-3861 or 800-441-1414.
www.fairmont.com/frontenac.
How does a hotel live up to
its reputation as a landmark
and national treasure? With
self-assurance and every resort
amenity, from spa to pool to tennis
court, all set in pavilions built over
generations—just like in a real
castle. Elegant, paneled salons
have welcomed prime ministers
and royalty, and the staff is trained
to extend equal deference to all
guests, whether they stay in one of
the standard value-priced rooms
or in an executive suite.
Casual **Café de la Terrasse** (**$$–$$$**),
with its river **views**, offers breakfast,
lunch, and dinner with a buffet as
well as an à la carte menu option.

Moderate

Auberge St-Pierre

$$ **51 rooms**

79 Rue St-Pierre.
418-694-7981 or 888-268-1017.
www.auberge.qc.ca.
Sedate and sophisiticated, the
St-Pierre incorporates new
rooms and suites built into the
structure that once housed
Canada's first insurance company.
The contrasting Art Moderne
fittings of other hotels in heritage
quarters are shunned here. Most
rooms have exposed brick walls,
hardwood floors, print curtains,

thick comforters, and reproduction furniture that together suggest old Quebec. Bathrooms are modern and Internet hook-up is provided.

Hôtel Le Priori
$$ **26 rooms**
15 Rue Sault-au-Matelot.
418-692-3992 or 800-351-3992.
www.hotellepriori.com.
On the trendier side of **Lower Town**, Le Priori fills a heritage stone building with a dignified stuccoed facade. It's located on a quiet street, a few blocks back from the river. Rooms vary in size, as well as fittings; some come with claw-foot tubs out in the open, others with modern showers. **Restaurant Toast! ($$$)** wraps around the lobby and opens into a private garden in warm weather; the cuisine is French.

Inexpensive

Hôtel Belley
$ **15 rooms**
249 Rue St-Paul.
418-692-1694 or 888-692-1694.
www.oricom.ca/belley.
With its rustic brick facade and steep roof pierced with gables, the Belley looks every bit the tavern and lodging house that it has been for over a century and a half. It's been spruced up with modern lighting and contemporary works of art, but the tin ceilings and floors of octagonal tile exude the Olden Days. In the rooms, metal and black-and-white wood tables, chairs, and beds play against exposed bricks and odd-shaped windows. The **bistro ($)** serves continental breakfast, micro brews, and sandwiches with **views** over the marina and train station *(VIA Rail)*.

Hôtel Le Saint-Paul
$ **27 rooms**
229 Rue St-Paul. 418-694-4414
or 888-794-4414.
www.lesaintpaul.qc.ca.
This brick Queen Anne structure, with all its original nooks, crannies, low windows, and exposed brick walls is located in the **Old Port** area of **Lower Town**, surrounded by antique shops. Features vary in the modestly priced rooms, but all have a full modern bath. **Restaurant Le Grill ($$)** is a light-filled Victorian salon that specializes in French cuisine.

Hôtel du Vieux Québec
$ **45 rooms**
1190 Rue St-Jean. 418-692-1850
or 800-361-7787. www.hvq.com.
Accommodation in **Upper Town** is pricey, but this wonderful exception features the charm of a 19C edifice and the feeling of being part of a vibrant Quebec City neighborhood. Large rooms have adequate comforts and some even have cooking facilities. Rates go down the longer you stay and rise to the $$$ range in summer.

Auberge Internationale de Québec
$ **62 rooms**
19 Rue Sainte-Ursule.
418-694-0755 or 800-461-8585.
www.cisq.org.
Quebec City's youth hostel is like a stay at a monastery. A fine and substantial house in **Upper Town**, without frills or embellishment, but comfortable enough, with polished wood floors and simple furnishings. An on-site café plus reading and games rooms encourage casual encounters. *Private and family rooms are available.*

155

The following abbreviations may appear in this Index:
LHN Lieu Historique National

INDEX

List of Maps

Photo Credits (page Icons)

Must Know
©Blackred/iStockphoto.com *Star Attractions*: 6-9
©Nigel Carse/iStockphoto.com *Calendar of Events*: 10-13
©Richard Cano/iStockphoto.com *Practical Information*: 14-23

Must Sees
©Pierre Étheir/MICHELIN *Neighbourhoods*: 28-36, *Historic Sites*: 37-43
©Perry Mastrovito/Age Fotostock *Landmarks*: 44-57
©Sophie Poirier/Musée du Château Dufresne *Museums*: 58-69
©iStockphoto.com/Vladone *Parks and Gardens*: 70-73
© Tourisme Montréal *Best Views*: 74-75
©Camirand Photo/Office du tourisme de Québec *Neighbourhoods*: 76-79
©Doug Rogers/MICHELIN *Lower Town*: 80-86, *Grande Allée*: 99

©Thomas Sbampato/Age Fotostock *Upper Town*: 87-96
©J. Beardsell/La Citadelle de Quebec *Fortifications*: 97-98
©Sébastien Larose/Tourisme Cantons-de-l'Est *Excursions*: 100-111

Must Dos
© Witold Skrypczak/Alamy *Sports and Activities*: 112-118
©ALEAIMAGE/iStockphoto.com *Kids*: 119-123
©Shannon Workman/Bigstockphoto.com *Performing Arts*: 124-127
©Jill Chen/iStockphoto.com *Nightlife*: 128-129
© narvikk/iStockphoto.com *Shop*: 130-133
© Subbotina Anna/Fotolia.com *Spas*: 134-135
©Marie-France Bélanger/iStockphoto.com *Restaurants*: 136-145
©Larry Roberg/iStockphoto.com *Hotels*: 146-155

INDEX